BÉATRICE FONTANEL & DANIEL WOLFROMM

JOURNEYS THROUGH LOUVRE ABU DHABI

اللوفر أبوظبي
LOUVRE ABU DHABI

ABRAMS | NEW YORK

SEUIL JEUNESSE

SUMMARY

↗ Hand axe, France, Indre-et-Loire, ca. 500,000–200,000 BCE, 20.5 x 14 cm, flint

→ *Mobile – Untitled,* Alexander Calder, United States, New York, ca. 1934, 62.9 x 88.9 cm, metal rods, painted wood

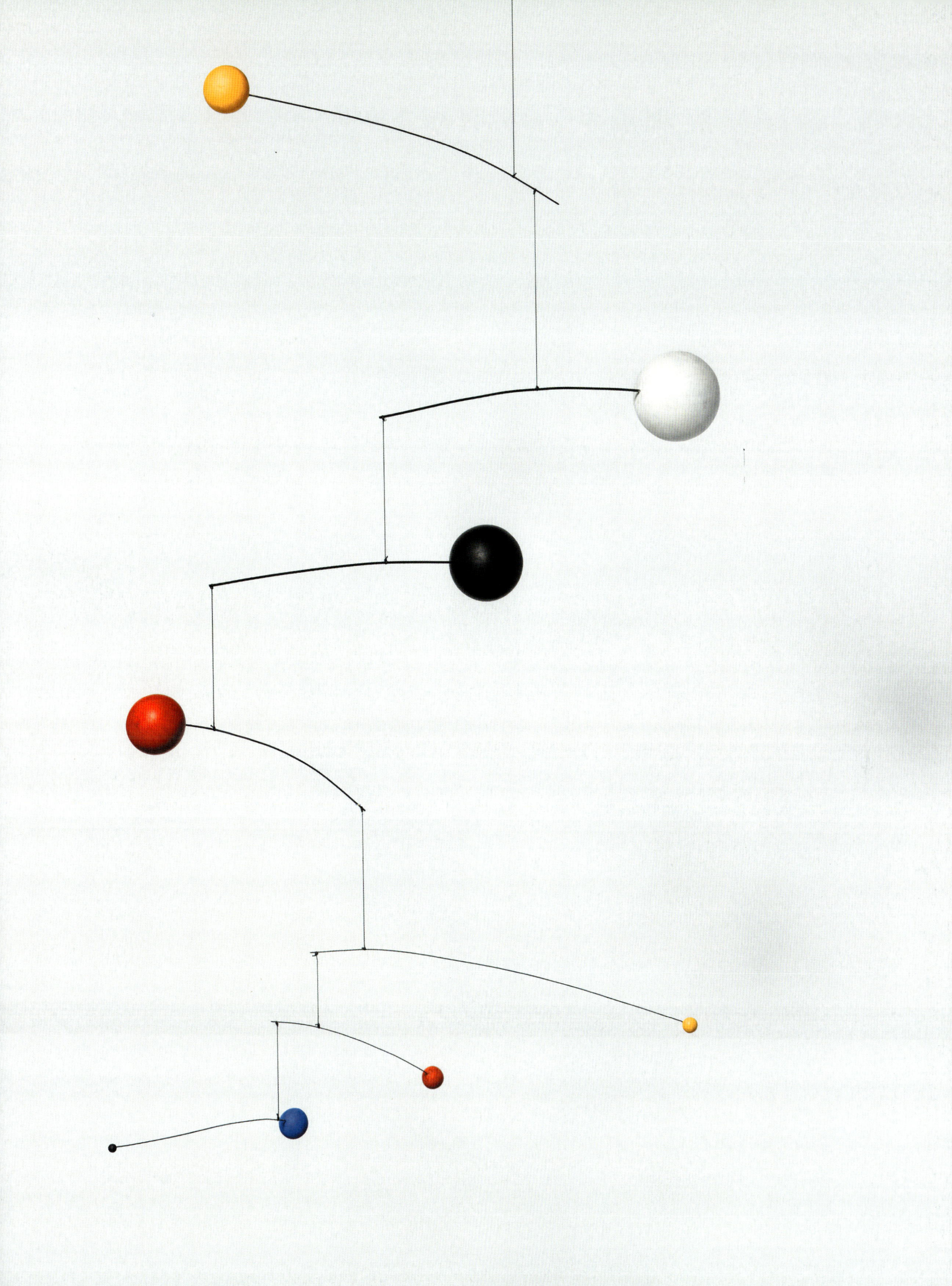

AN INVITATION TO TRAVEL

Ibn Battuta is one of the greatest explorers of all time. In the 14th century, when trade was vastly developing, he continually joined the caravans that trundled across Asia and embarked on Muslim ships. Louvre Abu Dhabi museum invites you to follow in the footsteps of this intrepid adventurer and depart alongside him for fabulous tours around the world, travelling back through the centuries as if in a time machine. You will learn that the great conquering civilisations, despite their often-Homeric battles, nonetheless influenced and enriched one another. And that far-flung civilisations, which never came into contact, curiously developed artistic styles with points in common. The museum's collections are designed to bring together works of art from cultures separated by the course of history and geography. Observe them closely and you will be amazed at what they reveal: secret understandings, born out of silent conversations that seem to share some common concept of universal beauty. Louvre Abu Dhabi is a meeting place for a medley of cultures and religions. Beneath its lacy steel dome, sheltered from the desert heat, you will discover the vast and unbounded immensity of human experience.

↗ A MESOPOTAMIAN ORANT (WOMAN PRAYING)
This orant with delicately clasped hands originally had big eyes, probably made of shells inserted into bitumen mastic, with perhaps lapis-lazuli gemstones for pupils. She wears the traditional *kaunakes*, a dress made from uniform strands of sheep's wool. The faithful would deposit these little statuettes in sanctuaries so that they might perpetuate the prayers of worshippers after they had departed.
Sumerian statue of a female worshipper, Iraq, 2800–2550 BCE, 36.2 x 13.5 x 5.7 cm, gypsum

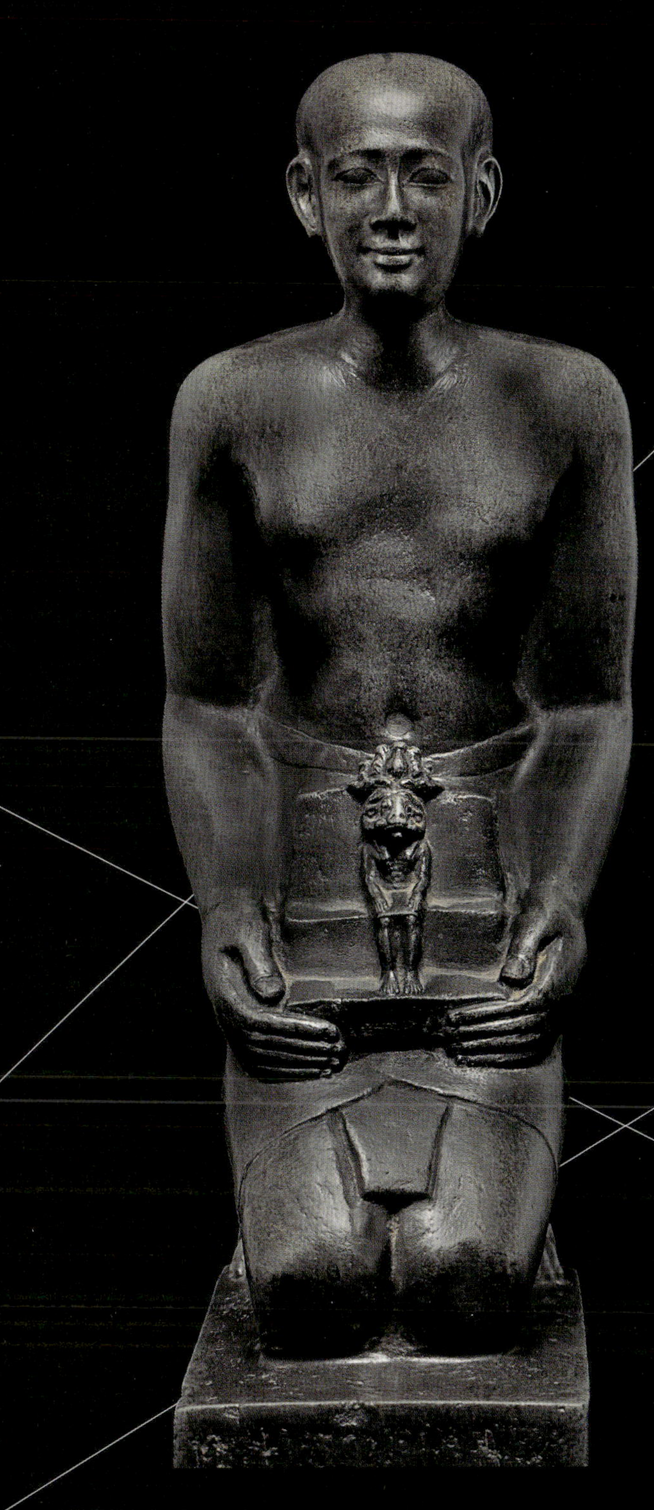

↗ EGYPTIAN ORANT
This orant-figure of a young Egyptian at prayer is holding the statuette of a god with the head of a ram, probably Amun, the chief deity of the Egyptian Empire – shown here seated on its throne and wearing the *atef* (crown of Osiris and the Pharaohs). From 664-332 BCE, Egypt saw various economic and military setbacks; but in terms of art, this was a richly fertile era, as evidenced by the beauty of this meditating orant with its smooth, elongated, egg-shaped skull typical of the period. It was the custom among certain elites in Ancient Egypt to deform the skull of newborn infants, elongating it intentionally in the belief that this would increase their powers of memory and learning. An elongated skull was seen as more beautiful – it was an embellishment.
Statue of a worshipper holding a seated god, Egypt, 400–300 BCE, 35 cm, greywacke

↗ FANG FIGURINE
This impressive female statuette formed part of a reliquary of the Fang people from southern Cameroon and Gabon. Reliquaries were designed as receptacles for the relics (skulls, bones, organs) of important people. Such figurines were inserted at the top of bark boxes and wicker baskets containing the relics of ancestors, revered and consulted before embarking on great journeys and important battles, or deciding where to locate villages.
Reliquary statue, Fang culture, Gabon, ca. 1900, 51 x 14 x 15 cm, wood

GODDESSES OR PRINCESSES?

Ten thousand years BCE, as the climate grew milder, human beings in certain parts of the world turned from nomadic hunter-gatherers to farmers. In stages, they began to raise livestock and plant crops, build villages surrounded by fields and fenced enclosures for their herds. So began the Neolithic Revolution, also called the Agricultural Revolution, which marked a slow but major transition in human history. As living conditions improved, the global population steadily rose and people sought to protect their crops, goods and ever-increasing wealth. This they did by building fortified towns.

→ The incised motifs represent the hairstyle, necklaces and belt of the two-headed figure. The small hole in each lobe was perhaps originally intended for earrings and the nose is almost beak-like. The marks on the face suggest tattoos or scarifications. A dual feminine deity, Siamese twins, a wealthy follower, a high priestess or an imaginary creature? Four thousand years since it was first created, the figurine remains an enigma, its function still uncertain.
Plank idol with two heads, Cyprus, ca. 2300–1900 BCE, 27.9 x 11.2 x 0.5 cm, polished and incised terracotta

Around three thousand years BCE, the world's population numbered barely 100 million people spread across the face of the earth. These days, it's hard to imagine such a world! Human societies isolated from one another by immense oceans and insurmountable mountain ranges nonetheless developed on all the continents – in China, the Middle East and Central America. During this period, striking statuettes were created, such as this two-headed idol and Bactrian idol.

In gratitude to their ever-bountiful deities, humans fashioned figurines symbolising fertility. Ever since Neolithic times, Mediterranean communities working the land had been mixing the local red clay soil with soft water. In Cyprus, they crafted plaques featuring a variety of revered creatures, which archaeologists later found in graves, together with other offerings such as vases, cooking pots and knives. The strange idol featured here, with one body but two heads, makes you think of Siamese twins. With their little eyes no bigger than pinholes, they seem surprised to see us. Pablo Picasso, who also sculpted figures with schematic forms, would certainly have loved them...

↘ **This fine lady with her delicate doll-like features was almost certainly an idol. Her dress is reminiscent of a *kaunakes*, the woollen mantel edged with fringes and tassels worn in Mesopotamia (located in what we now call Iraq). Mesopotamia in those days was the seat of a powerful civilisation located thousands of kilometres from Bactria, north of present-day Afghanistan.**
Woman dressed in a woollen garment: protective deity (?), Oxus civilisation, Central Asia, Bactria, ca. 2300–1700 BCE, 25.3 x 11.5 x 9.5 cm, chlorite, calcite

Bactria lay thousands of kilometres further east in Central Asia, a region with a wealth of natural resources set in the fertile lands that extend from the foot of the Himalayas. Watered by a major river formerly known as the Oxus (today the Amu Darya), Bactria was home to a flourishing civilisation that endured for six hundred years until it disappeared around 1700 BCE for unknown reasons. The valley also served as the only east-west passageway between India and the Middle East. It provided a trade route for caravans loaded with all manner of precious merchandise that stopped at the princely fortresses along the way to shelter with their goods. This fascinating masterpiece hails from that legendary land and depicts a Bactrian princess: one of the powerful goddesses that maintained order in the world, held the forces of darkness at bay and ensured the revival of vegetation in spring. It is carved out of a grey-green stone called chlorite (for the dress) and fine limestone (for the face). Despite the loss of arms and legs, it appears to have retained all of its mighty powers.

EGYPT, THE GIFT OF THE NILE

Without the Nile River, there would have been no Egyptian civilisation. In ancient times, the Nile regularly burst its banks, flooding the shores with waters rich in fertile silt. This meant that the local people could grow cereals, vegetables and fruit even though they lived in one of the driest places on Earth. The world's longest rivers – the Nile in Egypt, the Tigris and Euphrates in Mesopotamia and the Yellow River in Northern China – thus gave birth to the world's foremost civilisations.

Henuttawy was the daughter of a pharaoh. When she died, there was surely a funeral ceremony as for all Egyptian princesses. Her body had to be preserved through mummification and transported across the Nile on a funerary boat so that her sarcophagus and the treasures it contained could be laid to rest in the Valley of the Queens. But Henuttawy lived in the troubled times that marked the turn of the First Millennium, a period rife with intrigues, assassinations and power grabs. As the people went hungry, great care had to be taken to protect the royal tombs from looting. This explains why the beautiful Henuttawy was buried in three sarcophagi placed one inside the other like Russian nesting dolls. To trick thieves, the outermost coffin was made of wood and quite humble in appearance, like the next two. No one could have guessed that the innermost coffin was actually immensely valuable.

It was made of "cartonnage": a lightweight material produced from linen or papyrus, covered in plaster and richly decorated with gold. Nestled inside it like a chrysalis lay Henuttawy's mummy. So it is that this Egyptian princess with the look of a dreamy adolescent, her eyes of glass paste delicately outlined in black kohl, has been gazing at us wisely now for more than 3000 years.

Wealthy Egyptians liked be buried with everyday belongings in the hope that they could continue to enjoy their worldly goods in the afterlife. The miniature funerary boat pictured here is an exact replica of its full-scale, oar-propelled counterpart. Just 73cm long, it is no bigger than a large toy but still serves to remind us that the Egyptians were expert boat-builders and brilliant navigators – some of the boats built on the pharaonic construction sites were more than 60 metres long. This miniature is typical of the models commonly placed inside the tomb of the deceased: miniature villas and gardens, verandas, butcher's and baker's stalls, and weaving workshops complete with figurines holding tools. Together they represent a powerful testament to everyday life in Ancient Egypt. Rarely has an art form originally created for the nobility paid such a beautiful, life-like tribute to the labourers of society.

↓ Standing at the front of the barge is a man sounding the depth of the sandy riverbed, essential to avoid beaching in the marshes that teemed with short-tempered hippopotami. The coxswain at the rear meanwhile keeps the boat on course. Carried along by the current, the boat glides effortlessly through the water, mast down. On the return trip, the sail would be raised.
Model funerary boat and crew, workshops of Meir (?), Egypt, 1991–1785 BCE, 26 x 73 x 13 cm, wood lined with stucco and painted

↘ Henuttawy was protected by deities. Her chest features the goddess Maat, the personification of justice, order and balance, recognisable by the tall feather in her headdress. Also plainly visible are the solar discs of Isis, goddess of magic, love, beauty and joy; her sister Nephthys; and the four sons of the falcon god Horus.
Sarcophagus of Henuttawy: coffins and mummy wrappings, Egypt, 950–900 BCE, 163 x 38 x 31 cm, painted wood, stuccoed and painted cloth

PERSIAN ARCHERS AND GREEK WARRIORS

The coastline of Greece reaches into the Mediterranean Sea in a series of jagged spurs that seem to claw at the water itself. Its ports and cities were the cradle of an admirable civilisation that reached its zenith in Athens in the 5th century BCE. Meanwhile in the Middle East, Darius I, king of Persia and sworn enemy of the Greeks, built an immense empire that was epitomised by his archers, just as Athenian power was symbolised by the hoplite, or heavy infantryman.

↓ **The hoplite's face was almost entirely covered by his rigid bronze helmet, which must have been very uncomfortable, especially in hot weather. With its cheek guards, slightly flaring neck guard and slender nasal (nose protector), it is certainly forbidding in appearance. But it also has great physical beauty, and as such is sure to appeal to today's foremost sculptors.**
Military helmet, Greece, ca. 550 BCE, 26 cm, bronze

By the 8th century BCE, Sparta, Athens, Corinth and Thebes were constantly at each other's throats. Peace was but a brief respite before a renewed onslaught, allowing each city-state to rearm in order to consolidate its victory, or plan for revenge. Power was concentrated in the hands of the cavalry, which consisted of a select group of noble citizens. But around the 5th century BCE Athens witnessed the birth of a new idea: *demokratia*, or the democratic form of government henceforth adopted by the Ancient Greek city-states. Women and slaves were excluded, but all freemen were equal in the eyes of the law and entitled to have their say and participate in the debates held in the *agora* or public meeting place. From a military point of view, the noble cavalry made way for the hoplites: an elite infantry corps consisting of small bands of citizen soldiers who fought together as a group, known as a phalanx. Hundreds of men would advance in a close formation, all of them heavily armed, helmeted and armoured, wielding swords, javelins and spears. Each hoplite provided his own equipment – which didn't come cheap. Over time their helmet became an emblem and was depicted on everything from statues to coins and vases. The Middle East was meanwhile under the sway of another elite corps of warriors: the Persian archers. Dressed in richly embroidered tunics, the Persian archers formed part of the elite imperial guard of Darius I, commonly known as Darius the Great. The period between the 6th and 4th centuries BCE saw the Persian Empire extend its territory from the Mediterranean to the River Indus at the gateway to India. In tribute to the valour of the 10,000 men of his imperial guard – named the "Immortals" by the first Greek historian, Herodotus – Darius ordered the profile of one of his formidable archers to be struck on a coin as a symbol of his power. The archer seen here formed part of a colossal procession of Immortals, 100 metres long, that Darius commissioned to decorate the exterior facade of his palace in Susa. Together these Immortals perhaps represent an ideal image of the "Persian people" who were the cornerstone of his empire.

← This archer is part of a frieze made from coloured bricks depicting a stately procession of Darius' soldiers. His profile is unmistakable. He wears a long robe and beard; his thick curly hair is bunched at the nape of the neck and held back by a diadem of leaves. His hands are joined together on his spear, and he is carrying a superb quiver and large bow with duck beak ends.

Persian archer, Achaemenid Empire, Iran, Susa, ca. 510 BCE, 196 x 78.1 x 23.5 cm, glazed brick, Paris, Musée du Louvre

WILD BEASTS AND BIRDS OF SOLID GOLD

Gold, shining like the sun, was a sacred and highly coveted metal in Antiquity. For at least 7000 years, gold remained the preserve of kings, princes and deities, irrespective of differences in local culture. Rustproof, malleable and easy to work, this was the ideal metal for making jewellery and other adornments – those precious objects of power and wealth that their owners hoped to take with them into the afterlife.

In 1947 a bronze basin containing a hoard of gold objects was discovered by Kurdish villagers at the top of a long-ignored hill riddled with caves, near the ruins of the ancient citadel of Ziwiye (in present-day Iran). We know little about the site itself, except that an unknown prince chose to be buried there in the early 7th century BCE, together with his most treasured belongings (precious crockery, furniture and rich ornaments). This striking bracelet stands as a testament to his power and is plainly the work of a refined goldsmith. For the lions, its maker borrowed from the stylised motifs of Assyrian art to the west, and for the splendid gold-work, he took inspiration from the Scythian artisans of the steppes of Central Asia, in the north. Gold was rare in the Middle East but occasionally found in the form of flakes, in rivers such as the Pactolus, in the kingdom of the fabulously wealthy Croesus (present-day Turkey) or in the jagged veins of the Caucasus. Gold attracted tomb raiders of every type so it is nothing short of a miracle that this 3000 year-old jewellery piece has survived.

← This masterpiece of gold-working is fashioned at the ends into the heads of roaring lions, jowls retracted to expose their sharp fangs, perhaps to protect the four lion cubs resting beneath the bangle, and ward off any external threats to its princely owner. The heads were removable to allow the bangle to slip over the hand, then reattached with small nails.
Lion bracelet, Iran, Ziwiye, ca. 800–600 BCE, 6.7 x 9.5 x 8 cm, gold

Since time immemorial, princes, nobles and the wealthy have retained the services of great goldsmiths. These virtuoso creators were often inspired by figures of animals with great symbolic value, such as big cats, birds of prey and snakes. At the turn of the 5th century CE, Western Europe underwent a major upheaval following the deposing of Romulus Augustulus, the last of the Western Roman emperors. It was a time of great invasions and the end of the world as people as people knew it. The influence of the so-called "barbarians" from the east is plainly visible on this fibula or brooch with its powerful graphics depicting a bird of prey... You can almost hear the bird's strident call. The goldsmith who made it used a technique imported by the East Germanic people from the regions north of the Black Sea. Known as cloisonné (French for partition) it consists in creating a network of cells formed by tiny metal partitions. The cells on this fibula are inset with magnificent garnets from Gujarat in India, which testify to the fondness of these people for vivid hues.

↗ **Fibulae were worn by noblewomen and served to fasten their garments at the shoulder. This fibula, with its bird-like shape reminiscent of a falcon or eagle, was the very emblem of power in ancient times. The centre features a motif in the form of a cross – which became a symbol for Christianity. Twelve centimetres long, this fabulous piece of jewellery thus represents a fusion of ancient, barbarian and Christian traditions.**
Brooch in the form of an eagle, Italian peninsula, San Marino, Domagnano, 450–500 CE, 12.1 x 6.4 cm, gold, garnet

WINGED CREATURES READY TO TAKE FLIGHT

Never trust appearances... This sphinx, despite its strange smile, is not as friendly as it looks; but the dragon, under its terrifying exterior, is actually quite an easy-going fellow. These two chimeras, apparently straight out of a nightmare, were the central figures of ancient Greek and Chinese civilisations.

↓ The head of the dragon has the look of an alligator's snout and is surmounted by stag's antlers. Its body is muscular, with a crest of fang-like spikes running along its back. It has feline legs but the talons of a bird of prey, and its coat, whether fur or scales, is rendered by elegant dotted volutes. This is a unique masterpiece in terms of size and reveals a detailed understanding of animals, inspired by the precise work of the people of the Steppes at the frontiers of China. This muscular dragon, cast in bronze, is also an astonishing technical feat.
Winged dragon, Warring States period, Northern China, ca. 450–250 BCE, 48.5 x 67 cm, bronze

Originally, around 600 BCE, the sphinx was a benevolent creature combining the bust of a lioness, the angular, sickle-shaped wings of a bird and the head of a woman with long braided locks. Perched on a funerary slab, the sphinx was supposed to watch over the troubled souls of the departed, serving a protective role in Egyptian culture. But the sphinx that appeared in Greek mythology two centuries later bore a rather more alarming smile.

Indeed, she promptly strangled and devoured any passer-by who failed to solve her riddle, which goes like this: "What creature has one voice and walks on four legs in the morning, two at noon and three in the evening?" Only Oedipus got the answer right: "Man: as an infant, he crawls on all fours; as an adult, he walks on two legs; and in old age, he uses a walking stick." And with that, Oedipus won the freedom of the terrorised people of Thebes who until that point had been devoured one after another by the dangerous sphinx – which, now mortified, threw itself off a high rock.

Claws out, neck extended, muscles braced, he pounces. But not to worry... the winged dragon is a benevolent genie with a protective function. It's true that you would never guess that from his appearance. Unlike his Western cousin, the Chinese dragon turns out to be an auspicious creature – a sort of good luck charm and symbol of fertility. The Chinese emperor was always a "son of the dragon". Statues of winged dragons mounted guard over palaces and monuments in the days of the "Warring States": a time of unending wars and massacres that persisted until 221 BCE, the year when China was unified under the iron rule of its first Emperor, Qin Shi Huangdi.

As sculptors gradually foreswore the abstract figures that had prevailed for more than two millennia, rectangular, geometric and oval shapes made way for human faces with well-formed features. Some archaeologists argue that the inscrutable smile on the lips of the sphinx suggests the benevolence attributed to such supernatural beings. Others take the rather more prosaic view that it simply reflects the standard way of sculpting difficult areas of the face, in this case the space between the mouth and the cheeks...

Sphinx, mythological creature, Greek civilisation, Greece or Italy, ca. 600–500 BCE, 57 x 21 x 67 cm, limestone

THE EMPEROR AND THE YOUNG ROMAN CITIZEN

Such greatness, such power! The Roman Empire reached its zenith in the 3rd century CE, having conquered the entire Mediterranean region, Europe, the Middle East and North Africa. The Emperor made his power felt from northern England to the borders of Turkey in the east, and to the banks of the Nile in the south. But then came uncertain times, both inside the empire and along its borders.

The excavation of ancient Roman sites began during the Italian Renaissance, under the Pope or other ruler's authority, and involved artists and scholars alike. Later still, in the 18th century Age of Enlightenment, the Greco-Roman civilisation even became a benchmark, the universal model to be followed by all. Every effort was made to exhume the treasures of a glorious past. The Tiber, legendary river of Rome, yielded this enormous head of an emperor – the remains of a statue roughly four metres high! Made of semi-precious gilt bronze, it testifies to a person of high status. An impressive figure certainly, but a wrinkled brow and dreamy look suggest his concerns for the future of the Empire. The head dates from the late 2nd century CE, the end of the "Golden Age" that marked the prosperous reign of the first twelve Caesars. The Empire was always ready to assimilate the culture of the inhabitants of conquered lands, and to absorb so-called "oriental" deities into their own pantheon, worshipping the Egyptian goddess Isis side by side with the Greek god Apollo.

His thick curly hair and well-groomed beard testify to a man of high rank. He was perhaps one of the many "ephemeral" emperors who struggled to retain power following the assassination in 191 AD of the cruel emperor Commodus (the inspiration for the film *Gladiator*). So began the Roman civil wars, not to mention the Barbarian raids along the frontiers of the Empire.

Head of a Roman emperor, fragment from a monumental statue, Italy, Rome, ca. 200 CE, 44 x 34 x 35 cm, gilded bronze

In the Roman province of Egypt, the dead were represented in a realistic and sensitive way that was intended to honour their memory and also preserve the traces of Egypt's glorious past. The Egypt of the pharaohs had ceased to exist in 31 BCE when Rome defeated Egypt at the Battle of Actium. But its artistic traditions merged with those of the Roman civilisation. This "man with cup" is a splendid example. His funerary portrait was executed in his lifetime and must have offered a good likeness true to Roman tradition. He would not however be cremated like a Roman but rather embalmed in keeping with strict Egyptian tradition. Painted with coloured wax onto a wood panel, the portrait kept well in the dry climate until it was eventually cut down and recessed into the coffin containing the subject's mummy, in the manner of the timeless masks of the pharaohs. With his big hazelnut eyes encircled by dark rings, and his finger placed on the rim of his cup, could it be that this young man is expressing his nostalgia for earthly life?

↗ **The Roman tunic with purple trim shows that this was a dignitary of Egyptian, Greek or Roman origin. His short hair and forehead fringe are reminiscent of the Caesars' hairstyles of the period. The portrait is proof of loyalty to Rome and is probably that of a dignitary from the ancient city of Antinous, a cosmopolitan settlement on the banks of the Nile, 300 km south of Cairo.**

Funerary portrait of a man with a cup, Roman Empire, Egypt, Antinopolis (?), ca. 225–250 CE, 42.7 x 23 x 0.9 cm, wax paint on wood

The Orator wears the majestic toga of a rich Roman citizen of the 2nd century BCE. Nine hundred years after the founding of Rome, the Empire he lived in was at the height of its power, calm, prosperous and seemingly eternal. The Orator reflected the very essence of that Empire, possessing a gravitas or seriousness that was considered the supreme virtue in Ancient Rome. His magisterial eloquence earned him a place alongside the most important men in the city, and as a master of public speaking he turned out to be the ideal political tool. He is represented here as a mature and solemn Roman commanding respect, draped in marble folds that testify to the prowess of the sculptors of that period.

The Indian Bodhisattva, pictured here in meditation, also radiates an impression of stability. The Orator and the Bodhisattva (the future Buddha) are the emblematic figures of two civilisations, one Roman, one Indian, whose respective territories lay thousands of kilometres apart. But both are the descendants of the Ancient Greek civilisation, a heritage they shared thanks to the unparalleled conquests of Alexander the Great. As a child, the dream of this Macedonian prince was to win repeated victories and achieve the not inconsiderable aim of uniting East and West. In just 12 years, his armies conquered an empire unmatched in size that stretched from Egypt all the way to India. It would not survive the death of Alexander, known as the "Lord of Asia", in 323 BCE. But the Eastern world would become lastingly imbued with Greek culture – as evidenced by this statue of the Bodhisattva, from the Gandhara region at the gateway to the Indus valley. It is now more than five centuries since Alexander led his expeditions, but the art of these so-called "Indo-Greek" kingdoms reveals a fusion of cultural influences (from Greece, Rome and India) that gave birth to a fascinating art of great refinement.

↖ **Named the "Orator", the statue depicts a serious-looking man taking the measure of the audience come to listen to him in the Senate or the Forum. He is in his prime and wears a ceremonial toga, an ample and complex item of clothing. The toga's majestic drapery was deliberately sculpted to reflect the qualities of the wearer. Its intricate folds were the tangible expression of his words – well structured, fulsome and flowing like his ably argued rhetoric.**
Man dressed in a Roman toga, called "The Orator", Roman Empire, Italy, 100–150 CE, 169 x 59 x 40 cm, marble

↙ The earliest images of the Buddha in human form come from Gandhara (now Pakistan) and were sculpted in the 1st century CE. The Bodhisattva is a Buddha in the making, on the threshold of Nirvana and enlightenment. Released from all human passions, he gazes down at the world with a benevolent eye, his look as serene as tranquil waters.

Bodhisattva, an intercessor between the Buddha and his followers, Kushan Empire, Pakistan, Gandhara, Takht-i-Bahi or Sahri-Bahlol, ca. 100–300 CE, 136 cm, schist

DIVINE FIGURES IN SUFFERING AND IN DANCE

Deities are revered by the faithful all over the world; but their appearance, gestures and the manner of their representation differ depending on the religion. Jesus Christ, prophet and martyr of Christianity, is represented as a man of suffering, a man who felt close to others, a mortal among mortals who gave himself to humanity. The Hindu god Shiva, on the other hand, with his athletic body and two pairs of arms, is depicted as the Lord of the Dance who gleefully tramples ignorance beneath his graceful footsteps.

Jesus is shown with a profoundly human face, frail body and wearing a crown of thorns. He is recognisable by the wounds in His hands and feet that were inflicted by the crucifixion. He shows His wounded palms to prove to non-believers that He is indeed who He claims to be and has risen from the dead. In his side is the fifth wound where a Roman soldier pierced Him with a spear to make sure He was dead.

Lord Shiva meanwhile appears full of energy. Hinduism is a religion that has no prophets, no spiritual leader who intercedes with a single god on behalf of the faithful. The religion originated in northern India more than 3000 years ago and recognises three principal gods: Brahma, the creator god; Vishnu, the preserver god; and Shiva, the destroyer. Hindus are free to choose just one of these three deities for their own personal worship while still revering the other two. Shiva is also a healing deity and "Lord of the Dance" (Nataraja), dance being an art form as old as the world itself. Hindus believe that Shiva created the cosmos by dancing on Mount Kallash, a domed mountain in Tibet that reaches a height of 6638 metres. Air, fire, water and earth were born with each pose as he danced in tempo. But Shiva can also bring forth the spark that will destroy the world. Depending on his mood he can be creative one moment and destructive the next. He is depicted here stamping his right foot on the dwarf Apasmara Purusha, the symbol of ignorance and immortal demon of forgetfulness. In so doing, Shiva ensures the lasting protection of knowledge. His other poses connote such qualities as appeasement and the virtue of giving, his hand placed on the hip of his partner, the goddess Uma, or his arm resting on the back of his bull mount, Nandi (meaning joyful in Sanskrit). Hindu sculptors can choose from 108 different dance poses to represent Shiva...

← **This moving sculpture gives thanks to Jesus Christ and through Him, to the humanity of the Christian God. It invites the faithful to emulate the piety of Jesus and follow in His footsteps, to meditate on His sufferings and His resurrection from the dead.**
Christ Showing His Wounds, Germany (Bavaria) or Austria, ca. 1515–20, 183 x 57 x 30 cm, painted wood

↗ Shiva dances to the rhythm of the small drum in his right hand, symbolising the primordial sound of the creation of the universe. In his left hand he holds a flame signifying the spark of destruction. For believers, there is nothing frightening about Shiva because they know that destruction will be followed by liberation and the rebirth of the world. On his head, Shiva's chignon (bun) is enclosed in a diadem, which is characteristic of the ascetic (a person detached from material things) in Indian art.

Dancing Shiva, Hindu divinity, Chola Kingdom, India, Tamil Nadu, ca. 950–1000 CE, 83 x 47.5 x 24.5 cm, bronze

THE SPLENDOUR OF SACRED TEXTS

Sacred texts are not like other books. The "Religions of the Book" (with a capital "B") are Judaism, Christianity and Islam, so-called because each one refers to a specific sacred book: the Torah for the Jews, the Bible for Christians and the Quran for Muslims. For the faithful, these writings are the expression of the Divine Word but they are also a prayer book and a code of conduct – they direct the actions of believers according to the word of God.

↓ The double-page spread of this Torah consists of tiny Hebrew letters arranged in a geometric pattern. As is customary with Hebrew Bibles, the manuscript combines two texts. One is a psalm, here an exhortation to obey the Law, laid out in a diamond grid pattern. The other, in the centre and featuring two flowers, is the Masorah: a collection of notes designed to safeguard the accurate transmission of the text and ensure its proper pronunciation and recitation.
Pentateuch: first section of the Torah, Yemen, Sana'a, 1498, 34.6 x 29.8 cm, ink on paper

Over the centuries, the transcriptions of sacred texts were embellished and enriched to arouse wonder in the faithful and pay tribute to God. The most original example is micro-calligraphy: a minute form of writing that grew out of Hebrew (Jewish) calligraphy in the Middle Ages and became characteristic of sacred texts. It was adopted by the Jewish community in Yemen, one of the oldest in the world, dating back to King Solomon and the legendary Queen of Sheba in the 9th century BCE. The text here appears to dance and swirl at the whim of starry rosettes set into a grid background. It shows that passages of the Torah were not only designed to be read but also displayed and admired as works of art in their own right – in this case, an interlaced geometric pattern.

The Christian tradition allows depictions of God, Jesus, the Virgin Mary and, more broadly, people and animals. The Jewish and Islamic traditions, on the other hand, take the view that the reader should not be distracted by imagery. The miniatures in this Bible illustrate the opening of the Genesis creation narrative. The text begins with an ornate initial letter "I" for the Latin *In principio* or "in the beginning", which is illuminated with gold. Each vignette illustrates the seven days of the creation of the world. On the first and second days, "God created the heavens and the earth." Next He created the birds and other animals, followed by the Sun, the Moon and the fishes, and lastly by Adam and Eve. On the seventh day, "God rested from all His work that He had done."

This magnificent work of art is a large-format Quranic manuscript featuring copious notes in the margins. Written in blue and red ink, they testify to a detailed and critical study of the writings at the time of the Mamluk Sultanate, in Cairo and Damascus. Every surah (chapter containing verses) is preceded by the ritual phrase, highlighted in gold lettering: "In the name of Allah, the most Beneficent, the Most Merciful."

→ **"In the name of Allah, the Most Beneficent, the Most Merciful (...). Have We not made the earth as a cradle? And made the mountains as pegs? And We have created you in pairs and made your sleep as a thing for rest. And made the night as a covering, and have made the day for livelihood. And We have built above you seven strong heavens. And have made therein a shining lamp (sun). And have sent down from the rainy clouds abundant water. That We may produce therewith seeds, vegetation and gardens of thick growth." (Surate 78, An-Naba, The Tidings) With these poetic lines begins the last section of the Holy Quran. Rich editions like this were commissioned from illumination workshops by the Mamluk sultans and dignitaries of Cairo and Damascus as testaments to their piety and power.**
Section from the Quran, last volume, Juz' 30, Mamluk Dynasty, Syria, Damascus (?), ca. 1250–1300, 47 x 62 cm, ink, colour and gold on paper, leather binding

← **This luxuriously produced Bible is a testament to the importance of Paris as an artistic capital in the 13th century. The vignettes are embellished with branching plants and an amusing winged creature with the head of a demon known as a "grotesque". It is moving to think that it is now some 750 years since the artist drew these delicate vertical lines between the text frame columns.**
Gothic Bible in two volumes, France, Paris, ca. 1250–80, 29 x 19 cm, vellum (calfskin)

THE WISDOM OF THE BUDDHA

Behind all appearances, there lies a hidden reality, which is perceivable only if we liberate ourselves from illusion. Such, in essence, are the teachings of the Buddha, who lived in the 5th century BCE. Though he himself wrote nothing in his lifetime, his ideas and principles were gradually committed to paper by his disciples who then spread his word on their many pilgrimages across Asia.

The sutras are the most important Buddhist texts. They represent the collected teachings of the Buddha, whose name means "The Awakened One". In Sanskrit, the origin of all Indian languages, sutra means "thread" or "string", referring to the Buddha's thread of thought but also to the thread used to sew together the pages of the sutras. This Indian manuscript contains 8000 verses and is formed from a stack of 218 folios or *pothi*, which are fastened by a cord threaded through two holes pierced in each leaf. It is written on palm leaves and features an array of divinities with extraordinary powers, accompanied by little sanctuaries represented in the margins. Titled *The Sutra of the Perfection of Wisdom*, it is among the most important and oldest of all the Buddhist sutras. There are hundreds of other sutras, some no longer than a few lines, others extend to several volumes. But all of them purport to reveal the Buddha's discourse on wisdom and the conversations in which he took part.

Buddhist philosophy was transmitted to China by means of these pothi, which arrived with Indian pilgrims and left a lasting impression. They were the basis of the Chinese accordion books, which were made by folding a sheet of paper back and forth. It was Chinese artisans who perfected the paper-making process in the 2nd century BCE, thus providing a more practical, durable and cheaper alternative to mediums such as wood, palm leaves and precious silk. Paper also made it easier to broaden the distribution of the Buddhist sutras. This luxuriously produced accordion manuscript is painted in gold on indigo paper and contains the Sutra of Perfect Enlightenment. Divided into 12 chapters, it records the Buddha's answers to the questions of the Bodhisattvas (great sages), among them the renowned Bodhisattva, Manjusri, who stands humbly before the Enlightened One.

← The twelve protective divinities, with their white, green, yellow and blue carnations (undraped parts of the figure) are carefully painted. All of the colours remain as vivid today as they were nearly 1000 years ago. Each figure is depicted gracefully seated on a throne, wearing jewellery and sporting a complex hairstyle, the head slightly inclined and surrounded by a blue halo.
The Sutra of the Perfection of Wisdom, sacred Buddhist text, Pala Dynasty, Eastern India, 1191, 6.2 x 55.5 cm, ink and gouache on palm leaves

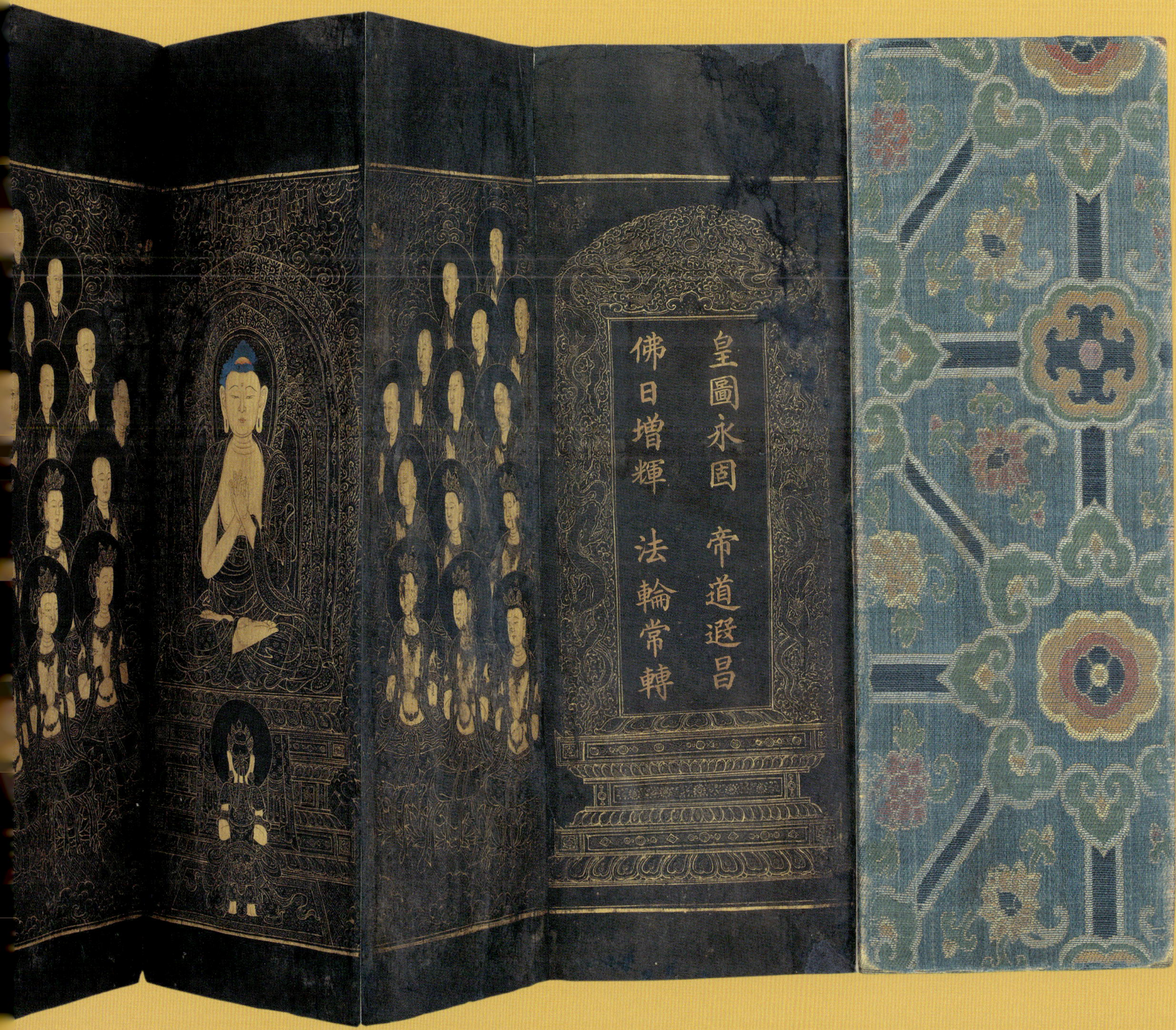

↓ Enthroned in the centre of this accordion book sits the Buddha, the spiritual teacher. He is surrounded by a crowd of disciples, divinities and Bodhisattvas come to hear his words. The decor, the characters and the clothing are drawn in fine gold lines, except for the skin of the faces and hands, which are entirely coloured in white plaster mixed with gold dust. This sumptuous sutra was probably commissioned by a person of high rank, if not a member of the Imperial Family.
The Sutra of Perfect Enlightenment, sacred Buddhist text, Yuan Dynasty, China, ca. 1350–1400, 32.4 x 190.5 cm, gold ink on paper

ADVENTUROUS CARAVANS ON THE ANCIENT SILK ROAD

Just as Europe was entering the Middle Ages, China was becoming the first world power – having already invented porcelain, paper, movable type and gunpowder. Around the 7th century CE, the country enjoyed a golden age in the reign of the powerful Tang dynasty and spared no effort to control the fabulous Silk Road so that it could export its riches to the West.

But the adventure actually began several centuries earlier with a network of important routes that were already used by caravans. It came to an end in the 15th century, with the decline of the Silk Road after nearly 2000 years of use. However, none of the traders who travelled the route knew it as such, since the term "Silk Road" only came into existence in the 19th century. They may even have been unaware that the roads they were using were part of this legendary route – this bridge between East and West for nearly a thousand years that facilitated the exchange of new ideas and precious commodities such as silks, brightly coloured carpets and ivory, carried on the backs of camels and horses. The sturdy Ferghana horse, known as the "heavenly horse", was bigger than any Chinese pony and played an essential role in Tang society. Because it could carry armoured men, the Ferghana horse brought glory to the Chinese cavalry. It also enabled the Empire to protect the long caravans laden with riches that trundled along the Silk Road, and ensure that news travelled quickly from one place to another, using the many relay stations along the way. These horses were imported from the Ferghana Valley in Central Asia for large-scale breeding. They were an animal figure much favoured by Chinese artists, not least because they made their owners proud. This ceramic piece is an example of a highly realistic funerary figurine called a *mingqi*. Like other cherished belongings, it was carefully modelled after the real thing – the faithful steed that would accompany its rider into the afterlife and continue to serve him there.

Another stoic animal from the arid steppes of Asia is the two-humped Bactrian camel. Thanks to its thick coat, it can withstand searing summers and severe snowy winters alike, and can go for long periods without water, eating only what it finds as it moves slowly but steadily on its interminable journeys. This Persian miniature likely originates from Qazvin and shows a camel chained to its owner. Qazan (in present-day Iran) was the first and ephemeral capital of the Safavid Empire of Persia and was known as the "city of reservoirs" due to the hundred or so reservoirs situated at the foot of the high mountains in the north. This made Qazvin an important staging post for the merchants who flocked to its tempting textile markets piled high with silk, woollen and cotton fabrics. The town thus enjoyed a privileged location on the Silk Road, connecting Europe and the Far East.

↓ **The camel's magnificent fleece stands out emphatically in this Persian miniature. Once shorn, it will fetch a good price for the camel master, who is seen here ostentatiously spinning the hair before the camel's eyes. Camel hair is used to make warm clothes, blankets and even tents.**
Wool Spinner and Tethered Camel, Iran, Qazvin (?), ca. 1560–70, 13 x 20 cm, ink, colours and gold on paper

↙ **The sturdy horse seen here is kitted out for polo, a team sport imported from Central Asia and very popular with the Chinese nobility. It is made of ceramic coated with a layer of glaze to give it a shiny appearance, make it waterproof and bring out its lovely colours. The horse's coat seems to have been carefully buffed up by its groom – originally its companion figurine but missing today.**

Bactrian horse,
Tang Dynasty, China,
ca. 618–907, 60 x 64 x 21.5 cm,
glazed ceramic

BIRDS OF A FEATHER FLOCK TOGETHER

There is a striking resemblance between these two ewers – you can almost hear them cackling in conversation. And yet they were separated by several centuries and a distance of more than 5000 kilometres. One features caramel-brown and moss-green tones and comes from Imperial China, the starting point of the ancient trading routes of the Silk Road. The other is turquoise blue and comes from the pottery workshops of Persia, which was an important stage on the Silk Road for the caravans that passed through carrying such precious ceramics.

Their similarity is no accident. On the contrary, Persian and Chinese artisans drew inspiration from their respective artworks – these ceramics passing along the Silk Road. The word ewer has a nice ring to it and comes from the Latin aquarium meaning "water place". It denotes an ornamental receptacle with a spout and handle, sometimes in the shape of a bird. Elegant ewers testified to the refined tastes of their wealthy owners. Chinese artisans had been masters in the art of ceramics for 5000 years and were constantly perfecting their technique. From 300 BCE, Chinese ceramics were fired in "dragon kilns": long, narrow tunnels, constructed on fairly steep hillsides. The rising heat served to cook large quantities of objects at temperatures exceeding 1200°C – temperatures that long remained unattainable by European potters. Under the Tang dynasty (618 – 907 CE), artisans perfected an original technique known as sancai: the mingling of three colours – brown, yellow and green – against a cream background, to produce an exuberant ripple finish that made ewers a great success. Ceramic ewers travelled along the routes of the Silk Road all the way to the Middle East and Europe. In exchange, the Chinese ceramicists of the Tang period took inspiration from the elegant shapes of traditional Persian ewers made of silver. So it was that artists adapted to the ever-changing tastes of their clientele. In the process, they built up a flourishing trade that made Chinese, Arab and Persian merchants very rich indeed.

In making this blue ewer, Persian artisans have pulled off a real feat: the production of a double-walled vessel. The inner wall is watertight while the outer wall is decorative, encasing the former in an openwork ceramic cage – rather like an elegant, snug-fitting corset. Ewers such as these were associated with the great themes of Islamic Iran. The cockerel announces a new day and wards off the evil eye; the openwork leaves arouse connotations of the giant, onomatopoeically named, *waqwaq* tree, known as the "talking tree", which according to legend bore fruit that looked like human heads and died if picked.

↗ The Chinese ewer has a spout formed like the head of a phoenix: the mythical bird that reigned over all other birds. Gentle and wise, the phoenix foretells momentous events. Its long tail serves as the handle. The tri-coloured sancai, waterproof glaze seems to flow over the flowers and rosettes that signify authority and dignity.
Ewer with a phoenix head, Tang Dynasty, China, ca. 600–900, 36.5 x 17 cm, glazed ceramic

↘ The cockerel's fixed stare and protuberant eye, encircled by concentric rings, is the guarantee of his protective powers. The body of the ewer is styled to resemble his paunch belly, and the handle his tail feathers. Inscribed on the neck and base are the following wishful sentiments: "I have held our love in the depths of my soul and discussed the slightest things with it, until the lover embraces the world to bring your love to it. May the Creator grant his protection to the owner of this ewer, wherever he may be."
Ewer with a rooster head, Iran, ca. 1100–1300, 29 x 16 cm, ceramic with painted underglaze, openwork decoration

ENCHANTING FRAGRANCES FROM THE EAST

Since the dawn of time, people have been making offerings of scented incense to the gods – the Canaanites to Baal, the Israelites to Yahweh and the Indians to Shiva and Ganesh. The Egyptian word for incense even means "to make divine". The Christians continued to make offerings of incense. When Jesus was born, the Three Wise Men came bearing gifts of gold, frankincense and myrrh. As the smoke plumes from burning incense rise slowly towards the Heavens, its purifying scent symbolises prayers ascending to the gods.

↗ This silver ball was used by the Chinese nobility to disperse incense. A small bowl was suspended inside on gimbals to prevent the burning incense from spilling. The chain and small hook were used to attach the ball to the wearer or to hook it to the canopy surrounding beds. At the court of Tang, incense was mixed with a huge array of other exotic fragrances such as camphor and sandalwood.
Spherical Censer, Tang Dynasty, China, 618–907, 4.3 cm, gilt bronze

The word "incense" covers all sorts of fragrant plant resins that are burned and come in various forms: raw resin; powder of resin, wood or herbs. They are fashioned in the shape of pellets, sticks and cones. Incense is a rare commodity, based on materials that are hard to extract. Some incenses are worth their weight in gold. In Ancient China, incense preparation became an art form as highly respected as calligraphy or the tea ceremony. Burning incense releases a subtle fragrance, combining scents of tree resins from the tropical forests of South East Asia, flowers and musk. Under the Emperors of the Tang dynasty in the 7th century CE, incense was burned in small, spherical censers finely crafted of silver. The ritual of burning incense was particularly favoured as an aid to meditation and mindfulness, and became part of the Buddhist ceremonies that were imported from India.

Then there was the Incense Road – a major trade route in Antiquity running from Yemen or the Sultanate of Oman to the Middle East. Incense resin was obtained from small trees of the genus *Boswellia* that grew on steep, arid hillsides. Tapping the trees produced a flow of milky sap that hardened when exposed to air, forming droplets up to several centimetres in size. Selected solidified droplets were then crushed to produce grains of incense. The resin eventually found its way to Mediterranean countries, carried first by boat across the Red Sea, then overland by caravans along trails fraught with danger. In Egypt, incense was used to embalm the dead before mummification, and burned at funerary ceremonies. Incense fumigation was also believed to ward off plagues – a view that persisted into Christian times when the use of incense showed no signs of waning. On the contrary, incense was put to good use

in the constant wars that favoured the spread of disease. In the early 16th century, Europe was rocked by the series of wars pitting France against the Holy Roman Empire, with towns and countryside everywhere savagely pillaged. But at the end of these wars, to illustrate the return to stability and give thanks to God, Bernhard Strigel, court portraitist to Emperor Maximilian I of Austria, painted this splendid representation of a scarlet angel. It is known as a thurifer angel (from Greek *thyos*, "incense" and Latin *ferre*, to "bear") because it holds a censer, which it swings energetically to disperse the fragrant smoke and purify the world.

↑ The European Renaissance marked a spectacular flourishing of the arts. German painters had a lively and expressive way of depicting the tensions of those troubled times. The angel pictured here, as an altar server vigorously swinging his censer, is a radiant representation of the heavenly guardian that mediates between God and human beings.
Thurifer angel, Bernhard Strigel, Germany, Swabia, ca. 1520, 65.5 x 78.6 cm, oil on wood

MINIATURES AND DELICATE IVORY LACE-WORK

Ever since prehistoric times, humans have been carving animal bones to produce everyday objects such as fibulae, buttons, combs, needles and fishing hooks. Smooth ivory from the tusks of elephants, on the other hand, was traditionally reserved for ornaments and ceremonial objects. In the West, the dawn of the Middle Ages saw craftsmen become increasingly skilled in the art of ivory carving, honing their talents to create graceful statuettes, dressing cases with mirrors for the elegant lady's toiletry items, and beautiful jewellery and perfume boxes...

↗ This little rounded box, or pyxis, is covered with carved ivory plaques and features a small lock to keep the contents safe. Decorated with a charming intermingling of plants and animals – deer, rabbits, birds – that testify to an Islamic presence in Sicily from the 12th century onwards that would have a lasting impact.
Pyxis with animal motifs, Italy, Sicily, ca. 1400–1500, 14.9 x 15.8 cm, ivory, copper alloy, Paris, Musée du Louvre

Few of these fragile objects have survived the troubled centuries untouched. This mirror-case, for example, is made of two ivory plaques that interlock. Concealed within these ivory covers was a polished metal mirror so ladies could look at their reflections. Carved ivory covers were a favourite with 14th-century courtiers and would be offered by the suitor to his ladylove as a token of affection. The delicate carving below shows a pair of lovers hunting with falcons (hunting being a metaphor for amorous conquests). Their charming appearance draws on the art of so-called "courtly love" and chivalric literature, which were very much in vogue at that time. The leaf motifs recall the enchanted forest, hunting scenes, magic potions and unrequited love, derived in large part from Celtic legends. One such is the tale of Tristan and Isolde who fled into the forest of Morrois to escape the jealous King Mark...

The allusion is quite subtle but the reference to falconry and the looks exchanged by the couple are enough to confirm their tender feelings. Toiletry accessories like this might also represent a game of chess, a gift of the heart, or the Siege of the Castle of Love. Around 1300, Parisian ivory carvers occupied a prominent place in Europe. And further south, the workshops of Sicily created ivory carvings that were no less refined

↘ The graceful young woman with a flowing dress feeds a falcon as she rides; her gentleman companion's gaze is piercing as he holds a falcon on his wrist. In the corner, a valet is sounding a hunting horn. Interlacing foliage surrounds this amorous scene suggesting the dense forest, and six mysterious creatures observe the lovers while a little dog trots on the ground. Falconry reached the Arab world from Central Asia in the 7th century and was adopted by the West in the Middle Ages. *Mirror case: hunting with a falcon,* France, Paris, ca. 1330–50, 10 x 10 cm, ivory

and detailed. Being the largest island in the Mediterranean, Sicily was a crossroads for its civilisations – the place where Muslim, European and Byzantine influences were woven together, as we see here in this ivory casket, which might once have contained precious stones, jewels or perfumes. Many other carved ivory items would have been included among the everyday belongings of noble families – statuettes, tiny boats, sundials, medallions, message cases, flasks, whistles, snuff boxes and more. With the passing of the centuries, the trade in ivory has been gradually banned by certain countries: by France and the USA in 2016 and China in 2017. But sadly, there is still a thriving trade in illegal ivory, with elephant populations in serious decline.

BIG LAID-BACK LIONS AND SMALL AGILE MONSTERS

Water is the source of life and a symbol of purity. The Greeks, Jews, Arabs and Hindus would all purify themselves with water, the Muslims through ritual ablutions, the Christians through the rite of baptism. People everywhere have always loved the refreshing sound of running water. As such, graceful ewers were exclusively produced for wealthy clients, not to mention the many canals, fountains and pools specially designed for palaces and shady gardens.

The lion, king of the animals and guardian of thrones, temples and tombs, was often associated with water, its presence symbolising the power of the property owner. In the Middle Ages for instance, when southern Spain was still under Muslim rule, the builders of the Alhambra, in Grenada, installed a magnificent alabaster basin in the heart of their palatial fortress. It is supported by 12 white marble lions symbolising the palace guards, and has a gushing water fountain as its central feature. From Spain to Egypt, many rich Muslim homes would have owned a vessel with handle and spout called an aquamanile. Used at table for pouring water, an aquamanile was a sign of a well-mannered and convivial host. In the 12th century, aquamaniles in the shape of lions found their way into the northern part of Christian Europe. Such water pourers nonetheless remain rare, but as examples of artefacts inspired by the Moors (Muslims) of Andalusia, they offer tangible evidence of trade across the Mediterranean basin between European and Eastern merchants.

↖ The handle of the vessel depicts a small animal leaping on the lion's neck and apparently emerging from its mouth. Bronze aquamaniles were luxury items in the Middle Ages, often originating in Germany and inspired by Andalusian art. The powerful emperors of the Holy Roman Empire encouraged trade and artistic exchange between East and West.
Aquamanile in the form of a lion, northern Germany, ca. 1200, 29 x 32 x 11 cm, bronze

This placid-looking lion is a 12th-century masterpiece in bronze from the Moorish workshops of Andalusia. Its design straddles Eastern and Western influences, suggesting it was created by travelling artists. With its stylised head and massive but elegant curves, this lion was long held to be a fountain spout. However, researchers have recently put forward the theory that it was an automaton that roared like a big cat thanks to a set of bellows that expelled air through a windpipe. But little evidence of such devices remains today. The princes of the time had a particular fondness for these amazing automata that so impressed their visitors. They were the work of brilliant scholars and skilled craftsmen who also designed mechanical birds that would chirp in the branches of enchanted trees...

↖ The body of the lion bears the mysterious marks of projectiles – probably musket pellets fired in troubled times that would have silenced our lion for good. But we can still make out the words engraved on its body: "Favour, benediction and tranquillity/ Peace, good fortune and prosperity/Honour and long life to its owner." Sadly, these wishes may not have been fulfilled...

Monumental Lion: An Acoustic Automaton (?), southern Spain or southern Italy, ca. 1000–1200, 73 x 81 x 45 cm, bronze

THE FLOURISHING WORKS OF SCHOLARS AND POETS

The Middle Ages saw the spread of literature and poetry thanks to illuminated books that were entirely copied and decorated by hand and destined for the privileged few. Encyclopaedias encompassed all that was known of the stars, wind, botany and animals… "There are only two sciences: theology for the salvation of the soul and medicine for the salvation of the body." This quote from the Prophet Muhammad clearly reveals Islam's keen interest in the medical sciences since its earliest beginnings.

Leaves, roots and flowers… This plant species is almost certainly a member of the thistle family, faithfully reproduced on paper from the original specimen. It features in a *Treatise on Plants* where every plant is shown with an accompanying description. Other pages illustrate how to harvest plants or prepare remedies. The work comprises a compendium of medicine and pharmacopoeia – or the art of preparing remedies based on medicinal plants, among them mugwort, camomile, iris, hyacinth and narcissus. Originally written in Greek, such works were translated, enriched and annotated by scholars of the Middle East. So it was that Arabic, together with Persian, became one of the foremost scientific languages, as used by the celebrated physicians Avicenna and Averroes, and the lesser-known scholar Istifan Ibn Basil. A Christian based in Baghdad, Istifan was also the first translator of the major work by the

← **Dioscorides' work stresses the importance of the direct observation of plants in their natural habitat. In his preface, he reproaches those chattering colleagues of his who content themselves with reading about remedies but have no first-hand experience themselves. This plant has been carefully reproduced by the scribe down to the last detail, together with Istifan Ibn Basil's translation (visible at the top of the page).**
Page from the pharmacopeia of plants, De Materia Medica, Iraq, Baghdad, Arabic edition, ca. 1200–1300, 25 x 16.8 cm, ink and paint on paper

1st century CE Greek physician Dioscorides: *De materia medica* (Latin for "Concerning Medical Material"). This five-volume treatise on the efficacy of 800 natural substances is the origin of modern botany. Most of them are unguents made from plants but wines and mineral-based potions are also included. For 1500 years, Dioscorides' work remained a standard medical reference in the Western and Arab worlds alike, representing a tool for learning but also a work of art.

What a thrill it must have been for the person – prince, monk or rich bourgeois – to read these illuminated books of the Middle Ages! One of the most famous examples is *Le Roman de la Rose* ("Romance of the Rose"), a poem of some 22,000 verses describing an amorous conquest filled with adventure, and twists and turns. The making of these precious books could take months if not years, working in the chilly writing room (scriptorium) set aside for the scribe, and bringing together the skills of painters, calligraphers and master craftsmen

← **The margins are decorated with bells, violets and wild strawberries; a little monkey sits astride a chimera with the head of a bird and the legs of a lion; and a blazon hangs on a tree. The miniature depicts the young hero's dream of his ladylove Rose.**
"In the twentieth year of my life, at the age when Love exacts his tribute from young people, I lay down one night as usual and slept very soundly. During my sleep I saw a very pleasant and pleasing dream [...] [that] which I begin here, it is the Romance of the Rose, in which the whole art of love is contained."
Romance of the Rose, a work of courtly literature, Guillaume de Lorris and Jean de Meung, France, Paris, ca. 1430–70, 29.4 x 22.5 cm, illuminated manuscript on parchment, f.1r

GENTLE MADONNA

The Virgin Mary gazes with infinite tenderness as her child tries to catch the edge of her robe. In the early Middle Ages, the cult of the Virgin, Mother of Jesus, reached an unprecedented intensity. Representations of the Virgin and child, also known as the Madonna, were everywhere to be found, in every conceivable form: as sculptures on the facades of churches and houses, statues erected at crossroads, or portraits commissioned by art patrons and religious orders.

↓ Mary's cheeks are rendered in a delicate pink, symbolising her purity. The artist plays on contrast by using dark tones for her robe. The infant Jesus meanwhile appears to be wiggling his toes – like babies all over the world.
Virgin and Child,
Francesco Traini, Italy,
ca. 1325, 66.8 x 60.5 cm,
tempera on wood panel

This veneration of Mary or so-called Marian cult found its most striking expression in Byzantium, in the Christian East. The artists there depicted religious events in the form of icons, which were as precious as holy relics (the physical remains of saints). Some icons were enriched with gold and finely painted, chiselled with a jeweller's skill and encrusted with enamels and gemstones. In the West, particularly in Italy, the faithful would marvel at the sight of these icons that glittered in the darkness of the church.

The Madonna in this painting of the Virgin and Child by the Italian painter Francesco Traini is quite literally bathed in gold. She is also the embodiment of "immaculate" purity, the eternal virgin preserved since birth from all stain of original sin. The chubby-cheeked baby Jesus looks with adoring eyes at his mother. Believers from all walks of life – rich merchants, peasants and beggars alike – would ask the Virgin Mother for her protection. So it is that Mary has come to be widely regarded by Christians as the Mother of God and Mother of all humanity. She also holds a place of honour in Islam, where she is known as Maryam.

Early in the year 1480, more than a century and a half after the period of the Italian icons, Giovanni Bellini was working in his father's studio in Venice. There, he and his brother Gentile painted several works destined for religious communities. Giovanni's many pictures of the Mother and child feature babies wriggling, trying to escape, sucking their thumbs or falling asleep. But the infant Jesus seen here is sitting quietly, propped up against a book symbolising the Scriptures. With a serious look on His face, He gazes at the Madonna dressed in her sumptuous red robe, with her delicate hands clasped before her much-adored son. The painting is representative of the early European Renaissance that placed the human figure at the centre of artistic inspiration.

↗ **Giovanni Bellini used the oil painting technique, which had only recently arrived in Italy and distinguished the works of the Venetian school. The intense red of the Madonna's cloak is highlighted by the dark black colour of the background – an unusual choice for this artist. The painting also hints at the Virgin Mary's green, finely pleated dress trimmed with gold. But then this was the time when rich Italian cities boasted one of the most luxurious fashion and textile industries in the world...**
Virgin and Child, Giovanni Bellini, Italy, Venice, 1480–85, 109 x 85 cm, oil on wood panel

THE AGE OF THE MATHEMATICIANS

In Renaissance Europe, the home of every self-respecting gentleman was expected to contain a work illustrating one or several of the seven fundamental scientific disciplines, which ranged from grammar to geometry and arithmetic. Artists such as Frans Floris represented these abstractions through allegory. Ever since Antiquity, allegory had taken the form of a beautiful, serious-looking young woman who personified the discipline in question.

Allegories owed their origins to the nine Muses of Greek mythology: the nine daughters, born on nine consecutive nights, of the union of Zeus and Mnemosyne, the goddess of Memory who gave a name to all things... Among them is Clio, muse of history; and Urania, "dweller in heaven", the muse of astronomy, often shown with a pensive look, holding a celestial globe and gazing serenely at the stars.

Melpomene, Calliope, Euterpe and Terpsichore are meanwhile allegorical personifications of the arts: respectively tragedy and chorus, poetry, music and dance. For centuries, that tradition remained unchanged in Western art. On the right of this painting by Frans Floris is the allegory of arithmetic. Aided by three studious helpers, she is shown doing her sums, her bright red robe draped Greek style around her body. Inherited from the Greco-Roman civilisation and the school of Pythagoras, mathematics was developed by Arab thinkers who appropriated algebra and Indian numerals. The word "cipher" comes from the Arabic *sifr* meaning "zero". The word "algebra" also has its roots in Arabic and means "connecting calculations". Arithmetic is thus the science of numbers and their powers. It forms the basis of mathematics: the science that studies the properties of these numbers and the relations between them. In Western Europe, arithmetic was one of the seven great "liberal arts". The paintings of the ambitious Flemish artist Frans Floris, among others, represented allegories of these liberal arts. His works were commissioned by such wealthy dignitaries as the banker Nicolaas Bjongelinck, who financed the merchants of the port of Antwerp. With a population of more than 150,000 inhabitants, Antwerp then was one of the largest cities in Europe, a hub for the trade of gold and silver and the spices brought back from the Americas and Asia. These were dangerous but highly profitable expeditions, made possible by compasses, astrolabes, caravels and sturdy ships – innovations that were designed and constructed based on arithmetic and mathematical calculations.

← Frans Floris portrays the allegory of arithmetic as a woman dressed in the antique style, writing numbers with a stylus as the moneychangers and merchants opposite her dictate their accounts. At their feet is a volume whose spine bears the name of the Greek philosopher and mathematician Pythagoras; and another book bearing the name of the prophet Abraham, credited with bringing knowledge of arithmetic to Egypt, from whence it spread to Greece. The blue borders of the lady's scarlet-red tunic are decorated with numbers – the Arab synthesis of such learning.
Allegory of Arithmetic, Frans Floris, Belgium, Antwerp, 1557, 146 x 250 x 9.8 cm, oil on canvas

ASTROLABES AND COSMOGRAPHERS

The early 16th century saw the emergence of courageous mariners under the command of the Portuguese explorer Ferdinand Magellan, who braved the fury of the oceans to accomplish the first circumnavigation of the world. Such perilous expeditions were made possible by unprecedented advances in technology that went by such fabulous names as astrolabe, compass, caravel and the Portolan charts – the first-ever decorative maps specially prepared for navigators, with ports shown along the way...

↓ Ever since Greek Antiquity, the definition of the word astrolabe has been "star catcher". With its multiple overlapping discs, the astrolabe was a two-dimensional model of the universe. It enabled navigators to measure the altitude of celestial bodies and tell the time according to the position of the sun and stars. Using the device, sailors could find their position at sea and establish the best course to steer. This astrolabe is the work of a Moroccan artisan – a worthy representative of great Muslim manufacturers, and the custodian of a tradition stretching back 1000 years.
Astrolabe, Muhammad ibn Ahmad Al-Battuti, Morocco, Meknes (?), 1726–27, 24.2 x 22 x 0.65 cm, cast brass, silver nails

The astrolabe remained the principal navigation instrument until the appearance of the sextant in the 18th century. It was developed by Arab astronomers in the 8th century, based on the writings and observations of the Ancient Greeks. The Arabs in turn transmitted their knowledge to Europe and the East, thus fostering the revival of the science of the stars in the European Renaissance. To avoid the complicated calculations required to determine the movements of the stars, astronomers also used volvelles or wheel charts: paper constructions consisting of overlapping discs that rotated in relation to a fixed point. Wheel charts were used by physicians too, believing that the movement of the stars influenced the workings of the human body. In fact, volvelles functioned very much like early analogue computers. The finest examples are contained in the "Emperor's Astronomy", a masterpiece of 16th-century printing dedicated to the Holy Roman Emperor Charles V. This huge book brings together a series of 55 superb volvelles, all hand-coloured by its author and printer, Petrus Apianus, a German mathematician, cartographer, astronomer and printer all rolled into one. In the book he uses dynamic illustrations of the volvelles to describe astronomical cycles, lunar and solar eclipses and planetary movements. His work drew further inspiration from the theory of epicycles perfected by Ptolemy, a Greek astronomer and astrologist who believed that the Earth was at the centre of the universe and all the planets revolved around it. However, one of the greatest geniuses of the period, the Polish astronomer Nicolaus Copernicus, would later show (albeit not without difficulty) that it is the Earth that revolves around the Sun and not the other way round...

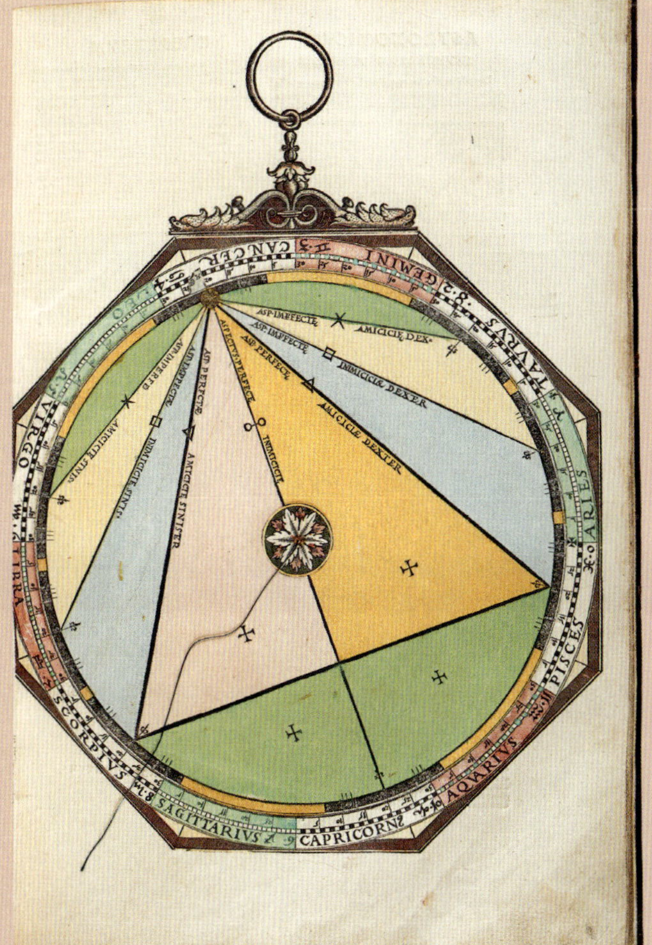

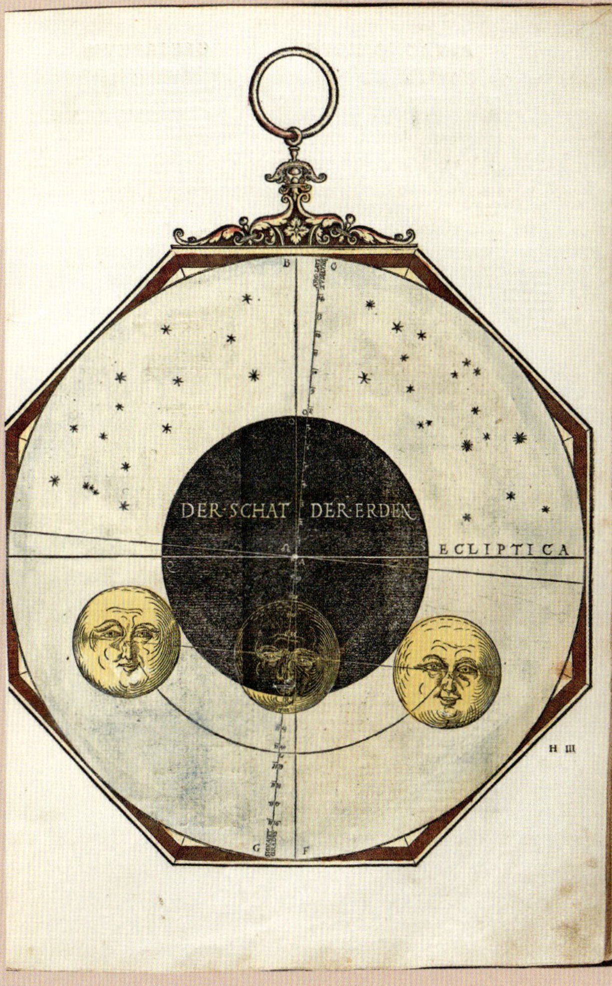

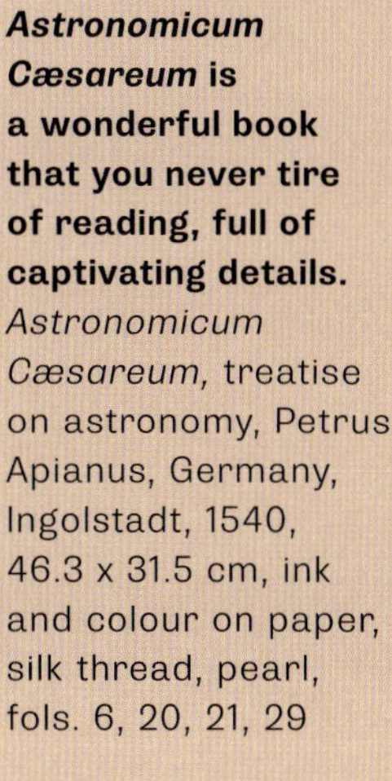

Petrus Apianus' *Astronomicum Cæsareum* is a wonderful book that you never tire of reading, full of captivating details.
Astronomicum Cæsareum, treatise on astronomy, Petrus Apianus, Germany, Ingolstadt, 1540, 46.3 x 31.5 cm, ink and colour on paper, silk thread, pearl, fols. 6, 20, 21, 29

Fabulous creatures and human beings spin around in a celestial whirlwind. In the centre, Hercules overcomes a monster.
fol. 6

A claw-foot dragon, tricoloured wings unfurled, points to the signs of the Zodiac with his face and tail: Scorpio, Sagittarius, Capricorn...
fol. 20

An adjustable isosceles triangle resembling a huge kite, designed for the purpose of triangulation.
fol. 21

Three moons and a black circle with the German words *"Der Schat der Erden"*, the shadow of the Earth, designed for eclipse calcuations.
fol. 29

SAILING THE SEVEN SEAS

The 16th century saw the monarchs, merchants and bankers of Europe finance great seafaring expeditions and commission wonderful "planispheres": representations of a spherical Earth showing the continents that remained to be explored. The race was on to discover new lands and the stakes were high. This little vessel certainly looks the part, but it had to settle for sailing in the confined space of this ceramic plate – the work of a Turkish potter from Iznik, a town widely renowned for its craftsmanship in the Renaissance. Rich families were expected to own elegant ceramic ware that would be brought out to impress their guests.

↗ **Guests of the Sultan of Constantinople (Istanbul today) were amused and delighted by Iznik ceramics, with their boat, flower and animal motifs. So too were the guests of the Italian merchants who eventually acquired Iznik ware. Amid swirling waves, fish pass under the sternpost of the galleon as the wind swells the sails and pennants. Painted on the bow and stern of the vessel, two wide-open eyes keep a lookout.**
Dish with a European ship, Ottoman Empire, Turkey, Iznik, 1625–50, 30 cm, ceramic with painted underglaze decoration

→ **Vesconte Maggiolo was ever ready to depict scenes of cannibalism in Brazil and giants in Patagonia, drawing on the accounts of the great Portuguese navigator Magellan. As in a cabinet of curiosities, realistic animals (elephants, lions and camels) rub shoulders with fabulous creatures (unicorns and giant snakes). The wind direction is symbolised by the breath of the god Aeolus, and the currents by small sailing ships wending their way between decorative rosettes.**
Planisphere, Vesconte Maggiolo, Italy, Genoa, 1531, 91.4 x 204.2 cm, vellum, ink, gold, silver, lapis lazuli

The vessel featured on this dish is probably an English ship, dating from the reign of Queen Elizabeth I, in an era marked by the spectacular growth of the English navy. The 16th century also saw the emergence of another great power: the Turkish Ottoman Empire, a vital crossroads between East and West. Ships of every kind from all over the Mediterranean – caravels, carracks, galleons – would stop at Turkish ports, stimulating the imagination of local craftsmen. Gradually however, nautical charts ceased to be centred on the Mediterranean. As the world grew bigger and new horizons opened up in the Americas and Asia, cartographers had their work cut out for them, with every European power eager to secure the services of the very best. The port of Genoa was a flourishing shipbuilding centre, and its cartographers led the market for portolan (harbour-finding) charts. In 1531 the Genoan Vesconte Maggiolo presented a more precise representation of the known world. Measuring two metres wide and one metre tall, the Maggiolo world map was not intended to be taken on board, but rather placed on a table where it could be read from all angles. The work says a lot about the political ambitions of the Republic of Genoa, then in the service of the French crown, which commissioned the map. As the official cartographer of the doge (the chief magistrate of Venice or Genoa), Maggiolo included all of the latest developments of interest to his masters' navigators. His map shows Africa and Arabia in detail but especially the northeast coast of America, with New York Bay marked for the very first time. We can make out India and the outlines of Asian archipelagos. At the heart of Africa is a coloured globe, and the Atlantic Ocean is already represented in proportion. The coats of arms of the competing powers of Castile, Portugal and France are scattered around the Americas while the King of Persia and Emperor of China are pictured beneath their baldachins, with Suleiman the Magnificent enthroned on a cushion.

JOURNEY THROUGH A JAPANESE SCREEN

In 1543, Portuguese merchants were the first Europeans to reach Japan, sailing from the south and landing in the Port of Nagasaki. The meeting between these two worlds henceforth became a favourite theme for Japanese artists, who were intrigued by the appearance of these unshaven, pointy-nosed strangers wearing curious hats and baggy trousers. From this came a new form of artistic expression called Nanban art, whose name derives from the derogatory term Nanban jin or "Southern Barbarians", as the Japanese unflatteringly dubbed these sailors whose appearance clashed with the Nipponese sense of refinement. This screen, rather like a picture book or cartoon strip, shows the Portuguese merchants unloading their cargo into small boats as the local people look on with curious eyes from the streets of the port. Portugal already had a firm foothold in India through its trading posts in Goa, and also in Macau – henceforth it could do business with Japan and compete with Spain's rival trading post in the Philippines. In exchange, the Japanese were happy to welcome Portuguese firearms and luxury goods such as Chinese porcelain, silks and elephants' tusks. On the left, is a three-masted carrack, its guns at the ready to defend the ship's precious cargo. On the far right, the captain has landed and strolls down the main street under the shade of a large parasol held aloft by a servant.

In Japan, screens served to keep out the sunlight and draughts in the fine houses of rich port merchants. Their gold panels might also reflect the lustre of the lights in the formal reception room. But the childlike simplicity of the picture you see here was totally at odds with reality. Japan at the time was being ravaged by civil war, and the Portuguese sailors who landed at the port had endured an interminable journey fraught with hardship at every turn.

Folding screens showing the arrival of Portuguese merchants in Japan, Japan, ca. 1625, 171 x 376.8 x 2 cm, ink, colours and gold on paper

THE REFINED ART OF PORTRAITURE

In Europe, during the Renaissance, the rediscovery of the art of Antiquity coincided with the dissemination of Greco-Roman science and philosophy. The Renaissance placed humankind at the centre of thought, marking the birth of Humanism. As the individual acquired a new sense of value, painters were no longer content to merely represent the social status of their sitters. They also sought to capture the personality and true nature of their subjects.

The princes, bankers and rich merchants of Europe's most prosperous cities commissioned paintings from artists, who in turn acquired a new status. The painter ceased to be regarded as a skilled artisan. He counted as a "master" – a virtuoso in the representation of the world and the human being. Leonardo da Vinci, for instance, sought to express the "reflection of the soul" in his portraits. The development of oil painting meanwhile allowed for an ever more refined rendering of details such as the play of light, facial expressions, and the texture of fabrics, as shown in this portrait of a young woman of African origin. Her soft eyes seem to be looking at us through the mists of time... Who is she? A lady's companion richly attired by her mistress? Perhaps a member of some wealthy family? Maybe Simonetta de Collevecchio, a freed slave who was rumoured to be the mother of Allessando de' Medici, Duke of Florence, known as *Il Moro* (The Moor)? One thing is certain: back then, it would have been rare to represent a young black woman dressed in the Florentine fashion of the day.

↖ The young black woman's apparel is typical of Renaissance Florence. So too is the beauty of her jewellery: black pearl earrings, coral necklace and silver headband holding her hair in place. She holds a clock in her hand that is clearly the work of a master jeweller. On her right, you can see the sleeve of a gown and a lace veil... The young sitter originally stood beside another woman who was the central figure in the painting. The painting was reframed at an unknown date, which only adds to its mystery.
Portrait of an African woman, Italy, Florence (?), ca. 1560, 60 x 39.5 cm, oil on canvas

↗ **Rembrandt wanted to show a new image of Christ. The face of this Jesus bears a meditative, almost dreamy expression that reflects His humanity and humility. His head is slightly tilted and suffused with divine light, which contrasts with His hair, dark red robe and the brown background. His clasped hands are barely sketched. What matters is His soft and gentle face.**
Head of a Young Man with Clasped Hands (Study of the Figure of the Christ), Rembrandt van Rijn, Netherlands, Amsterdam, ca. 1648–52, 25.5 x 20.1 cm, oil on oak panel

↘ **Thomas Wyatt the Younger, an English soldier and hero, is portrayed pulsating with life. Hans Holbein focuses on his youthful skin, his young and muscular neck, wispy beard, fine locks framing his forehead, and the depth of his clear gaze – as if he wanted to fathom the personality of this young man whose tragic destiny was to die a martyr's death.**
Portrait of Sir Thomas Wyatt the Younger, Hans Holbein the Younger, United Kingdom, ca. 1540–42, 42.5 cm, oil on wood

The patrons of Northern Europe also called upon the talents of great artists. The 17th century was the "Golden Age" of the Dutch mercantile republic, which was then the most prosperous country in Europe. By 1640, Rembrandt was at the height of his career and became deeply interested in the figure of Jesus Christ. He sought to give Him the face of an ordinary man at prayer, and is indeed said to have chosen his sitter from among the neighbouring Jewish community of Amsterdam.

Hans Holbein the Younger, court painter to Henry VIII of England, is the artist behind this portrait of a young Englishman. The painting shows the young man in profile, in the style of an antique medal, and is distinguished by those delicate lines characteristic of Renaissance art. The subject is Thomas Wyatt the Younger, an English rebel leader who was hanged and beheaded for treason at the age of 33. He is portrayed here as a martyr, with strained features, dark circles under his eyes and his gaze uplifted to the heavens.

SERVING UP ART

Ceramic ware, despite its fragility, was among the most traded goods in the world. The Chinese were traditionally the undisputed masters of ceramics, followed by the artisans of Iznik (located in what is now Turkey) who took inspiration from Chinese floral motifs to develop a style of their own – a style so appealing that it would in turn be imitated by Venetian craftsmen. Three centuries later, these ancient Turkish, Arabian and Persian designs would inspire British artists to create works of personal homage to the genius of Islamic art.

↗ **Reeds protect soils from heat and drought and also provide livestock and crops with shelter from scorching winds. This reed, with its broad leaves painted in a magnificent cobalt blue, forms a circle around the blooms and buds of the rose bush.**
Dish with a rose enclosed within a large saz-leaf, Ottoman Empire, Turkey, Iznik, ca. 1580, 30 cm, ceramic with painted underglaze

In the 16th century, Iznik craftsmen excelled in the art of ceramics, producing plates and dishes that graced the tables of the court of the Ottoman sultan. Flowers were not only decorative motifs, but also held powerful symbolic value. The three Iznik dishes pictured here share the same bright colours and motifs – the "four flowers" style, named after floral compositions of roses, tulips, carnations and hyacinth. All of these species grew in the gardens of Istanbul. The tulip, *lale* in Turkish, is an anagram of Allah, while the rose is associated with the prophet Muhammad. So it is easy to see why these floral compositions were so important to Muslims. No two decorations were ever alike – every dish was unique. Indeed in Turkey, where tulip bulbs were offered as gifts, everyone was expected to produce the very finest flowers. Throughout the Islamic world, from the Atlantic Ocean to the Bay of Bengal, the garden was considered a little piece of heaven on earth. It symbolised the celestial garden mentioned by Muhammad, in contrast to the untamed surrounding world, at the mercy of scorching heat and drought. The place of honour in the Islamic garden belonged to the tulip, which inspired such a fondness among the Dutch that by the 17th century the country was in the grip of tulip mania. Tulip bulbs imported from Constantinople triggered speculative buying completely out of all proportion with the value of the flower itself. In 1636, a single

↘ **Iznik ware featured flowers lovingly intertwined, seeming to almost flutter in a light breeze. This vivid tomato red was obtained by mixing the paint with iron oxide – a technique that earned Iznik craftsmen a reputation for excellence and made their ware a great success. Here, a precious speckled tulip with a bright blue colour vies for attention with the blue florets of the hyacinth, a symbol of prudence.**
Dish with narrow border, decorated with carnations and tulips, Ottoman Empire, Turkey, Iznik, 1570–75, 34.5 cm, ceramic with painted underglaze

→ **This dish is entirely given over to the spectacle of frilly carnations and speckled tulips that appear to want to grow beyond the limits of their confined space. Others show signs of wilting, their gently drooping heads a reminder of their fleeting existence. Craftsmanship in Islamic culture brought together the multiple talents of the craftsman as an artist but also a poet, as exemplified by the Persian Shah Quli (died 1556), who worked for the Turkish sultan Suleiman the Magnificent.**
Dish with four flowers, Ottoman Empire, Turkey, Iznik, ca. 1575, 28.3 cm, ceramic with painted underglaze

tulip bulb was worth 3000 florins, or the price of "two new carriages, two grey horses and a complete set of harness." This astonishing euphoria – the first financial bubble in history –collapsed dramatically seven years after it had begun in 1630, plunging Holland into a devastating depression...

In the late 19th century, with the industrial revolution in Europe moving full steam ahead, British artists who detested machines and the insatiable appetite for profit turned towards medieval and Eastern art. Their works were an immediate success with wealthy clients, whose daily lives were full of gloomy northern mists, just yearning for the light and bright colours of the East.

↗ **British artist William De Morgan liked to create fabulous universes, as evidenced by the two furious chimeras paired here, head to toe, preparing for a fight. Morgan was a founder of the Arts and Crafts movement that stood for traditional craftsmanship – handcrafts and manual techniques that were more rewarding for workmen than their factory counterparts.**
Dish with chimera, William De Morgan, United Kingdom, London, 1890–1900, 35.8 cm, ceramic, lustreware decoration

SOVEREIGNS IN MAJESTY FAR AND WIDE

Until the 19th century when they were ousted by machines, horses played an essential role. Vital to transportation and sturdy enough for hunting, horses also led soldiers into war. Cavalrymen on their steeds towered over the battlefield and the seething masses at their feet. In the 18th and 19th centuries, princes and kings wanted to be seen as warlords and unrivalled hunters, so they commissioned equestrian portraits from the finest artists of their time.

In 1762, Maharana Ari Singh succeeded to the throne of Mewar, a kingdom in north-west India that had been under the rule of the Singh Hindu dynasty for 200 years. But by then his kingdom was but a pale reflection of its former glory, constantly under threat from the Mughal princes who dominated Northern India, and by its neighbours, the Hindu monarchs of Rajasthan (which means "country of kings"). Ari Singh was also forced to cross swords with bands of marauders. Since the reign of the Grand Mughal Akbar in the 16th century, the so-called Marwari horse had been a symbol of valour and fiery spirit, said to remain on the battlefield until victory... or death. To express the prince's imposing character, this miniature shows him mastering his impetuous Marwari steed – the legendary "horse of heroes". The purpose of such miniatures was to make the stories in prose and poetry surrounding important figures more attractive and easier to understand.

← In the distance, you see elephants passing by, perhaps war elephants. But behind this edifying portrait, alas, lurks a less-than-glorious truth. Ari Singh's reign ended abruptly in 1773 when he was assassinated by his own mercenaries in the course of a hunting expedition.
Maharana Ari Singh II of Mewar (r. 1761–1773) on Horseback, School of Rajasthan, India, Kishangarh, ca. 1775–80, 22.8 x 15.5 cm, gouache with gold highlights on paper

Meanwhile in the West, Philip V of Spain, grandson of Louis XIV of France, was emerging as a key figure in early 18th-century Europe. At odds with the Austrian Emperors of the House of Habsburg, he found himself at the centre of a cruel conflict known as the War of the Spanish Succession. The ageing King Louis XIV decided that the young Philip could also assert his rights to the French throne. The prospect of a union between the crowns of France and Spain represented a *casus belli* (reason for war) for the Austrians, Dutch and English. So it was essential to create an image of Philip as a person of the utmost importance. This type of sculpture, with its combination of realism and allegory, was found throughout Europe, installed in the centres of squares and at major crossroads – a tribute to His Majesty King Philip, so people could see who was the man of the hour.

↗ **This statue of Philip V is almost an exact replica of the one of his grandfather, Louis XIV, the Sun King. He sports the same costume inspired by Roman Antiquity and even the same leonine wig, copied from those in fashion at the court of France. The only difference is Philip's face. The sculptor is Lorenzo Vaccaro, an artist from Naples, which was then one of Philip's many possessions.**
Equestrian portrait of Philip V, King of Spain, Lorenzo Vaccaro, Italy, 1702–05, 100 x 30 x 48 cm, bronze

THE OBAS, GREAT KINGS OF BENIN

For four centuries, equatorial Africa was dominated by the ancient Kingdom of Benin, in the south of what is now Nigeria. Its remarkable artistic metalwork gave rise to one of the greatest centres of African art. The development of this art was focused on the court of the Obas, the god-kings of the Yoruba people whose magnificent palaces so impressed Western travellers.

↓ **The royal altars of Benin sported many different styles of bronze roosters, each one carefully crafted to express its own personality – as if their makers had in mind a real-life rooster that they sought to portray through detailed handiwork.**
Altar sculpture of a rooster, Edo culture, Nigeria, ancient Kingdom of Benin, ca. 1700–1800, 42.5 x 41 x 18 cm, copper alloy

African trade was originally concentrated in the hands of Arab merchants who crossed the Sahara on route for the rich kingdoms of the South. There they exchanged their own goods for luxury products such as gold, ivory and spices. But Benin, being wide open to the Atlantic Ocean, also owed its fortune to the slave trade. Snatched from their native forests, local people were sold to European slavers who shipped them to America. Ife, the capital of the kingdom, saw its coffers swell. As did the cult of the dynasty of the Yoruba kings, whose representations were everywhere to be seen. An army of metalworkers, silversmiths, goldsmiths and sculptors worked on their behalf: an elite corps of artisans, gathered together in one part of town and commissioned by the Oba to decorate his palace. Weighed down with coral jewellery, the sovereign could barely move on ceremonial occasions and had to be held up on his rare excursions. His death was commemorated by a trophy-head made in bronze, a metal reserved for the royal family, which was adorned with sculpted brass plaques and placed on an altar at the centre of an immense palace constructed of wood. It would become an object of veneration during ceremonies, coated with a protective layer of ochre (red clay earth) that remains visible on certain sculptures that still exist today.

Roosters were used as sacrifices by the Yoruba people during rituals dedicated to their ancestors. This sculpted rooster was placed on an altar, like the trophy-head of the king, and paid tribute to *Iyoba*, the Queen Mother of Benin who possessed great powers and played a key role in her son's rise to greatness throughout her life. But the rooster could equally symbolise the king himself. The royal sculptors of Benin were famous for their artistry, combining a keen sense of observation with great technical skill and infinite patience... as expressed here in this plump-bellied rooster, apparently straight out of a cartoon, with its many delicate incisions that represent feathers. Of course, in Africa as on other continents, there were many different ways of expressing power. In the former Kingdom of Benin, for instance, the bronze trophy-head of the late king was placed on an altar in his palace as a reminder of his wisdom. It also held an engraved, upright, elephant tusk, a sort of illustrated chronicle of his exploits, so that his reign might be forever remembered.

↙ **The top of the pearly crown was designed to support a sculpted elephant tusk. Its base consists of a stack of necklaces reaching all the way to the king's lower lip, giving him a box-like appearance – but then the head was considered the seat of wisdom. Frolicking panther cubs feature at the base of his neck.**

Commemorative head of an Oba (king), Edo culture, Nigeria, ancient Kingdom of Benin, ca. 1800–50, 51 x 34 x 31 cm, bronze

MAGNIFICENT CABINETS OF CURIOSITY

The princes of the Renaissance liked to surround themselves with rare and precious objects that they collected and stored in their "study cabinets" – special areas set slightly apart from the grand reception rooms of their palaces. These were wealthy art patrons who commissioned craftsmen to create all manner of exceptional objects and furniture, which they fashioned out of rare species of wood, gemstones, mother-of-pearl and lacquer, imported from all over the world. This ewer and tabletop exemplify a real feat of technical ingenuity, comprising precious materials that fit together like the pieces of a jigsaw puzzle.

This ewer seems to come from a tale straight out of *Arabian Nights* and is one of the rare objects of this type that has survived in its original form. Combining Indian and Italian craftsmanship, the leaves are in finely worked mother-of-pearl and were assembled by a craftsman from the province of the Gujarat. It was then imported from India and embellished with gold by the virtuoso Neapolitan goldsmith Orazio Scoppa. Italy at the time served as an important crossroads between the empires of the East and West.

Opulent ewers like this, whether originating in India, Turkey or China, testify to an ever-increasing trade that by the 16th century included luxury objects specially made for export, such as sumptuous carpets and textiles, handsome furniture and other finely crafted items. Then there was the trade in Nature's own curiosities: exotic shells, strange creatures and monstrous stuffed animals. Sometimes these even came with fanciful stories attached. Hence the long-held belief that narwhal tusks were unicorn horns, which were worth their weight in gold and priced accordingly. The happy owner of this ewer remains a mystery, but we do know that this tabletop was commissioned by Francesco

← This ewer is covered with trilobal scales of mother-of-pearl and decorated with several rows of garnets and turquoises. The circular stand is made of gilded copper, as also is the placid-looking lion's head at the end of the spout. The handle features a woman's bust and the lid is topped by an amusing little duck wearing a crown – probably a reference to the family who owned this piece, whose identity remains unknown.
Indian ewer embellished in Italy, mother-of-pearl ewer: India, Gujarat; Italian mounting, attributed to Orazio Scoppa, ca. 1640, 42 x 33.5 cm, copper gilt, mother-of-pearl, turquoise and garnets

de' Medici, a member of the dynasty that ruled Florence, then one of the most prosperous cities in Europe. As patrons of art and science, the Medici family took advantage of their network of business connections over several decades to amass an extraordinary treasure trove of gems: big, blue lapis lazuli, red corallines and green jasper as speckled and veined as chunks of nougat. It took eight years to cut, polish and arrange the stones like the pieces of a jigsaw puzzle on a white marble table, creating a "picture in stone" that aroused wonder among the people of Florence. It was indeed a very rare work of art, not least for the sheer variety of valuable stones on display, each with a different colour, brilliance and opacity. Drawing inspiration from Eastern arabesque motifs, the tabletop pictured here was designed by the Italian painter and architect Giorgio Vasari, the founder of art history as we know it. The piece was admired by visitors to the Medici cabinet of curiosities, alongside other weird and wonderful items from the four corners of the world.

↑ The table and its top were never intended for use as furniture but as a masterpiece worthy of contemplation and rich with symbolism. It was commissioned by Francesco de' Medici, a man passionate about science, alchemy and architecture. Geometric shapes almost certainly held meanings for him that escape us today – subtle references to Francesco and his illustrious family. He could rightly take pride in the skills of his craftsmen as the hardness of these gemstones made them even more difficult to cut and polish than marble. Mounted with painstaking precision and perfectly intact, they have withstood the test of four centuries, their colours still as enchanting and vivid as ever.

Table Top known as *Tavolino di Gioie*, Bernardino di Porfirio da Leccio after a drawing by Giorgio Vasari, Italy, Florence, 1568, 160 x 107 cm, marble encrusted with semi-precious stones

STRONG EMOTIONS AND EXALTED VIRTUES

In the 17th century, European artists were commissioned by princes to create spectacular religious paintings pulsating with movement and colour – paintings featuring edifying stories that would strike the imagination of the spectator and appeal to their sensibility. The parable of the Good Samaritan and the story of Esther, for instance, are about generosity and courage. So it was that these two biblical characters, like the figures from Greek mythology, became timeless heroes. Virtuous and valorous, they set an example for us all.

The parable of the Good Samaritan tells the story of a kindly man who stops on his way to help a stranger: a young traveller set upon by bandits and left for dead. It is about loving your neighbour whoever that may be, and was told by Jesus in the Gospels, stressing that your "neighbour" could be anyone at all, in any situation. It harks back to the Golden Rule of the Old Testament: "Thou shalt love thy neighbour as thyself". In this painting by the Flemish painter Jacob Jordaens, the Good Samaritan, clad in a rich damask robe and wearing a heavy, oriental-style turban, gathers up the body of the unfortunate traveller, whose head is badly gashed. It is a moment full of drama. Every inch of the canvas is filled with movement: the characters seized with emotion; the worried-looking dog; even the horse, rendered in mother-of-pearl white, his long mane flowing in the wind. The overall impression is of a billowing theatre curtain.

↖ **Jacob Jordaens, the painter of this picture, is famous for his "heroic" style: strong composition, muscular forms, caressing light and a low viewpoint that draws the spectator into the joyful play of colours... The painter's generous style serves to express the idea of the Good Samaritan: the kindly, handsome man who places his hand on the back of the unconscious victim.**
The Good Samaritan, Jacob Jordaens, Belgium, Antwerp, ca. 1615–16, 185.5 x 173 cm, oil on canvas

Jean-François de Troy was famous in his time for historical, religious and mythological paintings but he also produced drawings that were used by the Gobelins manufactory to weave seven tapestries telling the beautiful story of Esther.
Esther Fainting Before Ahasuerus, Jean-François de Troy, France, Paris, 1730, 227 x 180 cm, oil on canvas

The second story, drawn from Jewish tradition and the Bible, is told in the Book of Esther. The name means "hidden" in Hebrew, as this wise and deeply pious woman hid her Jewish identity when she was living in the harem of the King of Persia. Through her courage, Esther would succeed in saving all of the Jews in the kingdom of Persia by revealing her religion and imploring her husband King Ahasuerus to prevent the extermination of her people by his Prime Minister Haman. As a symbol of piety and hope, Esther would come to be regarded by Christians as prefiguring the Virgin Mary. The spectator here is privy to an intensely emotional scene as the young Esther faints while imploring the help of her husband King Ahasuerus, who rushes to support her. The characters are presented in a theatrical setting, with Ahasuerus in the shadows and Esther in the spotlight, dressed in dazzling clothing dreamt up by the painter Jean-François de Troy, who in reality had no idea how people dressed at the court of the King of Persia in the 5th century BCE...

THE ARMOUR OF FIERCE CONQUERORS

Military equipment, like this fine suit of armour sported by the elite cavalry of the Ottoman army, was not only designed to protect its warring wearer. After peace was finally restored in the reign of the Tokugawa Shoguns, Japan's famous samurais were no longer obliged to fight. But they nonetheless commissioned dazzling suits of pageant armour for use on ceremonial occasions.

↘ **This suit of armour may have belonged to Nabeshima Yoshishige, who in 1707 became the chief of the Nabeshima clan, one of the ten richest families in Japan. The work of Master Armourer Miyata Katsusada, assembling these iron components was no mean feat, and the fact that this entire set of armour is still intact is quite exceptional. The articulated plates are held together by silk cord in kingfisher blue and overlap in places like scales to create an impression of embroidered armour. The helmet, with its iron mask, was designed to protect the head and face... and scare off adversaries too. Equally forbidding are the kneepads depicting heads of monsters. The breastplate meanwhile depicts a restless dragon.**
Armour of Nabeshima Yoshishige, fourth Lord of Nabeshima, Japan, ca. 1707–30, 190 cm, embossed iron, silk, gold, lacquer

With his two, golden antennae and hinged cuirass, the Japanese samurai looks somewhat like a giant crustacean. The paulownia flower adorning the helmet was the clan badge, and held great importance for the samurai warlord. The lofty appendages represent deer antlers and were designed to forestall blows to the head. Their height indicated the rank of the samurai and their particular shape – deer antlers, crab claws, rabbit ears, dragonfly wings and more – made the warlord easily identifiable by his men on the battlefield. Japan's seemingly endless feudal wars came to an end in the early 17th century when power passed to the Shoguns of the Tokugawa dynasty, the powerful military governors who would keep the peace in the now-unified Japan for the next two-and-a-half centuries (1603-1867). But the production of armour did not end with peace – far from it. Armour remained a symbol of power for high-ranking samurai with craftsmen competing to produce complex suits of armour like this one, based on evermore aesthetic and technically ambitious designs. Made of iron, copper, steel, lacquer and silk, samurai armour covered the wearer from head to foot while still allowing a certain freedom of movement.

This complete suit of Ottoman armour consists of a mail coat with reinforced metal plates that also allowed for movement. But unlike its showy counterpart, this was combat armour dating from the days when the Ottoman Empire was expanding far and wide. The fall of Constantinople in 1453 marked the end of the Byzantine or Eastern Roman Empire. Throughout the 16th century, on land and at sea, the sultan's army rose up against the Christian forces. It included 50,000 cavalrymen, among them the famous sipahis: heavily armoured, seasoned fighters who together formed a well-oiled war machine. Mounted on lighter steeds, the Ottoman cavalry relied on speed of attack, whereas Western cavalries opted to charge headlong into the enemy, astride large, powerful warhorses. Spade-shaped stirrups allowed the sipahi to fight standing in the saddle, sabre spinning in the air, while his heavier, Western opponent remained seated and altogether more static.

→ **The helmet's shape is typical of those worn by the warriors of the Ottoman Empire: the bulbous spiral imitates the folds of a turban, with a removable nasal that attaches at the front of the helmet. The knob at the top originally served to support an egret that has now disappeared. The body and face of the sipahi were protected by a coat of mail that extended to the eyes and provided protection for the nape of the neck. The horse's caparison (cover) consists of small, rectangular, highly mobile metal plates that must have made a rustling sound when the horse galloped.**
Armour for rider and horse, Ottoman Empire, Turkey, ca.1475 – 1525, 216 x 250 x 98 cm, steel, iron and fabric

VISITS FROM DISTINGUISHED AMBASSADORS

In the 17th century, as economic and diplomatic relations between countries intensified, ambassadors were despatched to distant kingdoms. Upon their return, these travellers on a mission would be full of wondrous tales about the splendour they had encountered in foreign courts. Sent to the mighty Ottoman Empire, the Austrian ambassador, dressed in his sumptuous finery, was likewise expected to embody the elegance and refinement of the West.

Eastern courts lay at the crossroads of ideas, art and fashion. So-called exotic chinoiseries and turqueries captivated Europeans' imaginations, inspiring artists to design new motifs for fabrics and wallpaper. In the north of India lay the dazzling court of the Great Mughal Emperor, as epitomised in the 17th century by the magnificent Taj Mahal: an immense mausoleum of white marble, studded with precious stones such as onyx, agate, jasper, turquoise and garnets, built by order of the Emperor in memory of his deceased wife. But following a century and a half of domination, the Mughal dynasty went into decline, freeing the way for European merchants to take advantage of the rivalries between Indian kingdoms. By 1815, when this gouache was executed, the Mughal Empire had collapsed and the British would soon colonise India. William Fraser was the English Commissioner of the Delhi Territory under the reign of the last Emperor. As a great admirer of Mughal culture, he commissioned Indian painters to represent the villagers, horse traders, dancers and also dignitaries attending court ceremonies. These spice-coloured pictures teeming with detail were much prized by Western art enthusiasts.

← **The cosmopolitan Mughal court brought together a great number of foreign dignitaries and as many national costumes. The Burmese ambassador, pictured here in the centre under an enormous, pastel-coloured parasol, wears a costume with an elaborate collar in the shape of the pagoda roofs of his home country. Beside him stand two Mughal officers dressed in the Islamic tradition of the Steppes. The Indian artist was also influenced by Western art, as shown by the three-quarter view faces, which was unusual for an Indian miniature.**
Burmese Ambassador to the Mughal Court, India, Delhi, 1815–20, 32 x 27 cm, gouache and gold on paper

Jean-Étienne Liotard focused his attention on the fabulous finery of the Austrian Habsburg Ambassador, who holds a letter of accreditation in his hand signed by the Sultan Mahmud I. His attire is extraordinarily lavish, fashioned out of fabrics such as glistening brocade and silk with pearly highlights. His hat is topped with peacock blue feathers, with stockings to match. *Count Corfiz Anton Ulfeldt in an Ottoman Interior*, Jean-Étienne Liotard, Turkey, Istanbul, 1740–41, 31.3 x 22.7 cm, gouache and watercolour on parchment

"Never allow yourself to paint without Nature as your reference – an art in which you excel." Geneva painter Jean-Étienne Liotard would bear those words in mind in 1736 when he embarked on a five-year journey that took him first to Italy then Constantinople. He was received by the Ottoman court, adopted Turkish costume, grew a long beard and soaked up the local culture. He continued to travel upon his return to Europe, where he earned the nickname "the Turkish painter". He even appeared in Turkish dress before the Empress Maria Theresa. You can't help thinking that it was deliberate mischief on his part to depict the Ambassador of Austria decked out like a Christmas tree.

THE SPIRIT AND POETRY OF CALLIGRAPHY

The art of fine writing, calligraphy, was viewed as the expression of a highly cultured mind in the Muslim East, also in China where it denoted a genuine man of letters, a "man of property". In Japan, the Grand Masters of the Kano School, so-named after a family of artists, took inspiration from Zen philosophy and its emphasis on meditation, becoming experts in brushwork and ink line drawing. Calligraphy was widely considered a major artistic accomplishment.

In Japan, the Kano School founded by Masanobu Kano (1434–1530) would dominate the art of painting and calligraphy for more than four centuries. Such a long-standing record is unique in the history of art. Brush strokes on fine silk are the essential characteristic of this tradition, whose principal exponent in the 17th century was the artist Kano Tan'yu, named official court painter to the Togukawa Shoguns. He portrays the habit worn by the monk Bodhidharma using rapid, loose brushstrokes that almost give the impression of an ideogram. The delicate treatment of the monk's bushy eyebrows, bulging eyes and grouchy expression indicate that this was indeed the legendary founder of the Zen School of silent meditation, who was famous for his gruff demeanour. The inscription at the top of Bodhidharma's portrait is by another monk, Chinese in this case: Yinyuan Longqui, the leader of another Zen sect in Japan. On the right, are the two sides of a miniature by the painters of the court of Lucknow, a great city in the north of India where the genre was revived by a group of artists who abandoned royal and literary epics in favour of scenes depicting the private lives of princes, at home in their palaces. In the 18th century, these delicate paintings became a favourite with European art connoisseurs, who placed large orders for miniatures with their fellow European travellers and collectors. Among them was Swiss colonel Antoine-Louis

From the age of sixteen, artist and calligrapher Kano Tan'yu (1602-1674) was the official painter in residence at the Shogun's palace. His style is unmistakable here, characterised by an economy of means and restrained elegance that reflects the Zen philosophy of his time. It contrasts with the wealth and prestige of his school, which served the court of the powerful Tokugawa clan.

Bodhidharma, Monk and Founder of Zen Buddhism, Ekuin Fugai, Japan, ca. 1600, 133.5 x 72.7 cm, ink and colour on paper

The back of the opposite illustration features a love poem hand-scripted by Muhammad ʻAli. The floral border draws inspiration from the Indiennes fabrics that were very fashionable in Europe at the time, providing an elegant frame for miniatures while also lending consistency to an otherwise rather disparate set of images.
Page from a Polier album (back): Calligraphed love poem, Mohammed Ali, India, Lucknow, 1780, 45.7 x 61.5 cm, gouache and ink on parchment, gold highlights

This depiction of conviviality in a garden proves that Persian and Indian artists were in full command of the European rules of perspective. As if in a sylvan theatre, the scene opens on a parterre filled with young women in saris, talking and smoking the hookah (or narghile), They are surrounded by female servants, musicians and dancers whose silhouettes are reflected in the water basins. In the background, the gardens stretch out as far as the eye can see, with two boats passing by on the horizon.
Page from a Polier album (front): Entertainments in a Garden, Muhammad Ali, India, Lucknow, 1780, 45.7 x 61.5 cm, paper laid on album page, ink, gouache and gold

Polier, one of the foremost dealers in miniatures. As a young man he joined the British army and entered the famous British East India trading company, before offering his services to a "nabob" (a governor at the court of the Mughal Emperors), then taking command of an army in the pay of the Mughal Emperor. Thanks to his knowledge of languages and the Hindu religion, he was able to gather precious information and gain admission to the inner circles of the imperial elite. On his return to Europe in 1788, he brought back a rich collection of muraqqa: albums containing miniatures of all shapes and sizes, mounted on sheets of card and framed by wide borders decorated with flowers, arabesques or sometimes flecked with gold. Among them was this scene of conviviality set in an immense garden, with, on the reverse side, a calligraphed love poem, surrounded by garlands of flowers.

SHIMMERING INDIAN PAINTINGS

The Maharaja, mounted on his elephant, charges ahead like a warrior on the battlefield as he prepares to strike a deathblow to the tiger. The Mughal miniature was meant to exalt the prince's strength. These two figures meanwhile, leaving a town double-quick on their camel, feature in a Punjabi folktale that is still told and sung today. In the 18th century, these two expressions of Indian art, one aristocratic, the other popular, proved equally irresistible to European art enthusiasts with a passion for so-called "oriental" miniatures.

In the Age of Enlightenment, Indian and Persian miniatures fascinated Europeans, appealing to their taste for novelty. English and French alike relished the opportunity to discover these arts and traditions from distant and as yet little-known lands. Little magical glimpses into the Orient, these images were an invitation on a journey, illustrating tales and legends that enchanted their collectors. People were moved by the tragic destiny of Prince Punnhun and his beloved Sassi, who was ready to overcome all obstacles separating her from her husband. But Punnhun's father and brothers opposed his union with the lovely Sassi on the grounds that he had married beneath his station. After many twists and turns, Sassi died of thirst crossing the endless desert to be with her husband. The tale condemns the cruel tradition of forced marriage, where the family takes the lead and thwarts the personal desires of lovers.

← **A brother of Prince Punnhun whisks him back to the family home astride a camel running at full tilt. In the distance, his lonely wife awaits him in his palace for their wedding night. The tale remains very popular in India as in Pakistan, but what interested Europeans about this miniature were the delicious details: the camel harness, the characters' clothing, jewellery and other accessories like the small flask, and even the two blossom branches and bevy of rabbits running away from the dog...**
Punnhun is Taken Away from his Wedding Night by his Brother, India, Jodhpur, ca. 1830–40, 28.9 x 20.8 cm, gouache with gold highlights on paper

↑ **This scene of tiger hunting showcases the monarch on his splendid elephant, which is richly decorated and bound by gold chains that control his movements. Galloping alongside the monarch are the beaters, followed by his bodyguards, one of them carrying the royal insignia. In the bottom right-hand corner, a rider takes the opportunity to spear a boar. Hunting scenes were part of the legend of the young prince who triumphs over the savagery embodied by the tiger, protecting his people and ruling over his land.**
A Royal Tiger Hunt, India, ca. 1800, 49 x 69.5 cm, gouache with gold highlights on paper

This miniature illustrates a scene of tiger hunting, drawing on the tradition of Mughal painting that focused primarily on the court life of rajahs and maharajas. The objective was to depict them in all their magnificence: at royal audiences surrounded by courtiers; at the head of gigantic processions of elephants and musicians accompanied by fireworks; or on hunting expeditions that proclaimed their stamina and virtuosity. Such was the taste for these "imageries" that a whole new industry arose under the guise of The Company School: workshops devoted to the production of Indian miniatures commissioned from local artists by the British East India Company, one of the major players in colonial trade. These little paintings in their spice colours found a ready clientele among European merchants and civil servants, combining traditional Indian style with the European taste for "exotic" scenes, sumptuous finery, unusual accessories and fairy-tale architecture. Many of them also depicted trades such as laundries, butchers, fishmongers and basket makers, and would often be bound into albums called muraqqa. But the arrival of photography in the mid-19th century spelled the end for these workshops, as people came to prefer the camera to the brush as a means of revealing the world and its mosaic of peoples.

JAPANESE PRINTS: CAPTURING THE EPHEMERAL

This lovely musician is also a patient mother, who smiles as she turns to look at her child tenderly nestled in her kimono. The 18th century brought a long period of peace and prosperity that fostered the development of the art of the Japanese print: a printmaking technique based on wood engraving. The artist Utamaro is considered one of the foremost exponents of the genre. His fellow artist Shunshō meanwhile depicted some of the most celebrated actors of Kabuki, the traditional form of Japanese theatre that greatly appealed to city dwellers in search of pleasure and entertainment. His images were widely reproduced, much to the delight of the actors' devotees.

The year 1600 saw the birth of a Japanese art movement that would endure for 250 years, making it a record in the world history of art. Its name was *Ukiyo-e*, which translates rather prettily into "pictures of the floating world". Artists would offer their prints to a clientele of erudite enthusiasts who appreciated the poetry of these images – wind and rain on a bridge, travellers in the snow, nervous carp at the bottom of a pond... Around 1665, the Japanese writer Asai Ryōi alluded to these new aspirations: "Live only in the present moment, give yourself up entirely to the contemplation of the moon or cherry blossom (...) never allow yourself to be crushed by poverty or let your expression betray poverty, rather drift down the river like a calabash carried by the current..."

When making a print, the artist first drew his design on thin paper, which the engraver then attached to a block of very hard wood such as cherry or catalpa. Next, he scooped out the parts left blank using a steel gouge, so leaving a design in relief on the block. The final step was to ink the block and press it down on a sheet of paper to make the print – which could be reproduced hundreds of times. Such

← This lovely head of hair required a delicate openwork treatment that must have been a real challenge for the engraver! The young mother tries to play the shamisen (three-stringed instrument) while her child clings to her arm. Her beautiful face is inspired by Naniwaya Okita, a servant in a teahouse and Utamaro's favourite model. Oval face, slightly inclined head, straight nose and half-open mouth: Utamaro always sought to capture the likeness of his subjects. Despite the challenges of the art form, he succeeded thanks to all the tiny details that make a person instantly recognisable and even give a hint of their personality.

Young Mother Playing the Shamisen, Kitagawa Utamaro, Japan, ca. 1798, 39 x 25.7 cm, ink on paper

↘ Katsukawa Shunshō was the designer of an album (called an "accordion book") that brought together images of actors on stage. He was a member of the Toril studio that for many years specialised in Kabuki theatre scenes. Actors interpret their roles in outrageous ways, some more outrageous than others depending on the character, much to the delight of the audience. This actor is pictured straddling a bull that is being led by the ring in his nose – an unusual image certainly, though shows featuring bulls were not uncommon in Japan. Accordion books often included the programmes of theatre or opera productions.
Actors of the Kabuki Theatre in their Roles, Katsukawa Shunshō, Japan, Edo, ca. 1750–1800, 31 x 13.5 cm, ink and colours on paper, f.16

works were modestly priced and enjoyed great success in the Edo period (1600-1868), so called after the new capital, now renamed Tokyo. With more than one million inhabitants, Edo was already one of the largest cities in the world. Orders for prints came flooding in as people increasingly appreciated these pictures that depicted places to stroll, entertainment and everyday life. Other favourites were the prints used to promote theatre performances, featuring actors in magnificent costumes striking ostentatious poses. Katsukawa Shunshō breathed new life into the genre by striving to capture the likeness of star actors in his portraits.

By the end of the 18th century the art of printing was at its zenith. The painter Utamaro was famous for his *bijin-ga* or pictures of beautiful ladies; Hokusai and Hiroshige were acclaimed for their unforgettable landscapes and images of the passing seasons. These works would also hold a fascination for the Impressionist painters. Eventually they were eclipsed by photography and modern printing techniques. But their influence is still felt today in popular culture – manga and cartoons being good examples.

THE CHARMS OF FAMILY LIFE

The 18th century saw French and English aristocrats alike develop a growing taste for the pleasures of family life. So much so that they wanted to be portrayed at home, surrounded by elegant objects, in private apartments that enjoyed a new level of comfort and offered a more intimate setting than grand reception rooms. As the individual acquired more importance, artists were commissioned to paint faithful representations of high-ranking couples. In India, on the other side of the world, touching family scenes also testified to this new taste for the private realm.

From Asia to Europe, by way of the Indian Ocean, foremost artists were commissioned by prosperous middle-class merchants grown richer still thanks to the expanding trade in precious exotic goods. Indian princes meanwhile wanted the same freedom of action and thought as their European counterparts. So it was that the 18th century saw a gradual move away from old-style images of military conquests and epic stories, in favour of images depicting the home life of Indian nobles. Mughal and Rajput artists were commissioned to paint scenes of pleasure, music and games, such as this picture of a man kneeling before his wife, who turns away as if displeased. But she can't help smiling at the antics of her son, who has just unravelled his father's turban as he straddles him like a horse.

← **The painters of miniatures were open to the world, and mixed Indian influences with inspirations from Persia and Europe. They created figurative scenes of private life in a delicate, almost feminine style. Here, distraught white birds fly against a darkening sky in the distance, heralding the monsoon – the bringer of the rains so long-awaited by farmers.**
Family at Play, Pahari School, India, Kangra (?), ca. 1800, 19.5 x 13 cm, gouache with gold highlights on paper

You can tell from their expensive clothing and the richly draped pink taffeta curtain that the aristocratic Welby couple were comfortably off. The fact that they are playing chess, then all the rage in London, also shows that they were in touch with the latest trends. But mystery lurks behind this image of the happy couple, captured here on canvas at the end of their game. You wonder about this lovely, pale young wife, staring out at us in her pearl necklace and white satin dress, and what her husband is thinking as he stands beside her with his right palm outstretched. Do their still youthful faces, turned towards the viewer, conceal some secret sentiments? Only two kings remain on the chessboard: is this the sign of a successful marriage between equals or of silent opposition? Francis Cotes, one of the most fashionable portrait artists of his day, leaves it to our imagination. In fact, Penelope Welby died quite suddenly in 1771, just two years after this painting was delivered.

↖ **The refined décor, comfortable surroundings, and thoughtful game all suggest a change in mentality among the upper and middle classes of this Age of Enlightenment in Europe. The role of women changed. Here, Penelope's elegance is easily equal to that of William, her husband. She is represented as a woman also capable of discussing new ideas and advances in science.**
Portrait of William and Penelope Welby Playing Chess,
Francis Cotes, United Kingdom, 1769, 135 x 152 cm, oil on canvas

IMPRESSIONS AND IMPRESSIONISM

Photography was a major invention of the mid-19th century, equalled only by the development of the steam engine. This was clear to exponents of the Impressionist movement such as Édouard Manet, Edgar Degas and Gustave Caillebotte. Reality, as captured through the lens of a camera and carefully framed by the photographer, entirely overturned their own artistic perception. *The Bohemian* by Manet, with his dark, staring eyes, fixes his gaze on the artist as if amused by posing for a painter for the very first time. Caillebotte's card players, on the other hand, appear so oblivious to his presence that it's as if they might have been caught unaware on canvas.

In fact, *The Bohemian* is a fragment of *The Gypsies*, a larger painting by Manet featuring this young musician standing with his back to a man drinking from a pitcher without touching it to his lips, alongside a woman with a baby in her lap, and a basket and garlic cloves at her feet. In the cafes and faubourgs (neighbourhoods) of Paris were gathered artists and transients who led a bohemian lifestyle and seldom ate their fill. In the eyes of the bourgeoisie, representations of vagabonds, servants and courtesans were vulgar and crude. Manet could not have cared less and painted anything he liked. But being a man of forceful character, he did not take kindly to criticism and would sometimes cut up his paintings in a fit of rage. As he did here, reframing this young musician who looks all the better for being alone with his noble bearing worthy of an Italian Renaissance prince. The critics said that Manet's style was too loose, even botched. Dignitaries who commissioned Manet to paint their portrait were not always pleased with the results. The *Salons* (official French art exhibitions) would too often reject his paintings… Traditional portraiture was intended to exalt the sitter and was a favourite with academic artists. But for a modern painter like Manet,

← Manet and his young associates shared a common interest in Spanish painting. In 1865 he took advantage of a brief stay in Madrid to visit the Prado Museum, where he admired the paintings of Vélasquez and Goya. His portrait of the bohemian reflects that Spanish influence. Manet painted his subject in the manner of the Impressionists, using quick, bold dabs of paint like his friend Claude Monet. He employed contrasting colours: a dark brown jacket slung over the shoulder, white shirt, bright yellow bandana against dark hair. The overall impression is of a broad-brush image, almost a snapshot.

The Bohemian, Édouard Manet, France, Paris, 1861–62 (cut out in 1867), 90.5 x 55.5 cm, oil on canvas

portraiture presented an opportunity to rejuvenate his art. Eventually the critics would come to acknowledge his talents and by the end of the century; Manet finally won recognition as a major precursor of modern art. Gustave Caillebotte also wanted to depict the realities of individuals in their environments, earning himself the label "realist". He willingly portrayed subjects such as clotheslines, people under umbrellas or a man taking a nap. Working-class scenes, such as carpenters stripping a wooden floor (*The Floor Scrapers*), came as easily to him as scenes from bourgeois life, which were more familiar being himself the heir to an immense fortune. Here he adopts the viewpoint of a person quietly watching a card game, being careful not to disturb the players. It's so silent you could hear a pin drop. But Caillebotte leaves us free to interpret the painting in any way we choose. Is this a group of friends enjoying themselves, or is it a routine event typical of boring, bourgeois entertainment?

↖ **The composition of Caillebotte's painting is quite precise. All eyes are on the green baize of the card table, with the exception of the man sitting behind on a sofa. The scene takes place at 31 Boulevard Haussmann in Paris, in the luxurious apartment of Gustave and his brother Martial, a pianist and composer (on the right of the picture). Gustave himself was mad about art, boats, yacht racing, stamps and botany. Eccentric certainly, but generous to a fault and with a fortune at his disposal that he regularly used to help his Impressionist colleagues. Upon his death, he bequeathed 67 paintings by Cézanne, Degas, Manet, Monet and Renoir to the French government.**
The Bezique Game, Gustave Caillebotte, France, Paris, 1880, 125.3 x 165.6 cm, oil on canvas

ASTONISHING TRAVELLING PHOTOGRAPHERS

People on their travels always loved to create little pencil drawings or watercolour paintings as mementos of the landscapes, monuments and characters they encountered along the way. With the arrival of photography in 1839 came an exciting medium that hobbyists embraced as a new way to record the sights they admired on their trips. Taking photos in those days was not an easy thing, but nothing deterred these pioneers of the new art of photography.

Wealthy adventurer Joseph-Philibert Girault de Prangey was an excellent draughtsman and early daguerreotypist. He probably learned the technique from Louis Daguerre himself, the French photographer who gave his name to a photographic technique that was an immediate hit with the rich and privileged. By 1841 Paris was in the grip of "daguerreotype mania", with sales that year exceeding two thousand cameras and half a million plates in the capital alone. Prangey meanwhile set off on a four-year journey around the Mediterranean that would yield the very first photos of the Middle East. Comprising 900 pictures, they included images captured in Palestine and also the Dome of the Rock, a Muslim holy site in Jerusalem. Shot in 1844, the image is tinged with grey and golden brown and is now extremely valuable. For Prangey, photography involved travelling with a cumbersome dark room laden with copper plates; coating these with silver before taking the shot, then exposing the plates to an iodine solution; developing the resulting images over heated mercury; and finally, "fixing" them in a bath of hyposulfite of soda. The equipment

← This delicate lace laid flat on photosensitive paper is a "photogenic drawing" – an image with much of the precision of a stencil or contact print. Talbot worked on the process for five years before perfecting it in 1839. He hoped it would interest the textile industry as a means of making copies of lace patterns. But still life images like these have a strikingly poetic dimension that goes far beyond a faithful reflection of inert objects. Talbot was an erudite scholar, passionate about mathematics, astronomy, chemistry, linguistics, botany and the arts. He spoke several languages and was also an accomplished artist.
Lace, William Henry Fox Talbot, United Kingdom (?), 1840–45, 23 x 18.8 cm, salted paper print

← **Looking at this picture by Girault de Prangey, you sense his passionate interest in Arab-Muslim architecture. His photograph shows Jerusalem's Dome of the Rock framed to show off its splendour. But as daguerreotypes could not be reproduced in a book, he made a drawing of the image, which he then had engraved with other images in order to publish them in a collection, brought together in all their finery. However the book was eventually too expensive and only included some 20 illustrations recording his long journey around the Mediterranean. Sadly, the publication was a flop.**
Jerusalem. The Grand Mosque, Joseph-Philibert Girault de Prangey, Jerusalem, 1844, 12 x 18.8 cm, daguerreotype

was expensive and unavailable on location. The process was long-winded, complicated and tricky to manage. And it did not permit the printing of duplicates, as there were no negatives. For all of these reasons, within about 10 years the daguerreotype technique had been superseded by photographic prints on paper, which were reproducible and far less costly. Their inventor was the accomplished British scholar Henry Fox Talbot. In 1839 Talbot perfected a way to create an impression of an object by placing it on a sheet of writing paper sensitised with silver nitrate. It was then exposed to sunlight, which acted on the bare areas, creating a negative image of the shapes left masked during the exposure time. Hence this image of Chantilly lace thanks to the magic of chemistry. The result just as common with Talbot's other creations – winged seeds, ferns, insect wings – is nothing short of magical. In generating multiple positive prints from negatives, Talbot's process is rightly considered the forerunner of modern photography.

In the late 19th century, photographers wanted to convey a different view of the world – an objective perception of reality that contrasted with that of the painters. They wanted to capture reality as it happened. These days everybody knows that photography is just as subjective as painting – you see the world through the eyes of the photographer. This picture of a young Egyptian woman carrying a water jar, looking as lovely as a statue from Antiquity, was taken by an unknown photographer who clearly possessed all the artistic sensibility of his painterly counterparts.

↑ **Gracefully posed, the young woman holds a heavy water jar with one hand, the other one rests on her long jellabiya, its sombre tones contrasting with the whiteness of her skin and surroundings. The photo is composed with all the care of a painting and the young woman's pensive look hints at a mysterious eastern tale.**

ORIENTAL REALITY VERSUS ORIENTALISM

Venturing across the seas has always captured the imagination. In the 19th century, Romanticism and Napoleon Bonaparte's military expedition to Egypt provided inspiration for Western artists to discover Eastern lands shrouded in mystery. Their so-called "orientalist" paintings fuelled the fantasies of Western audiences and fostered exchange with some Eastern artists, who trained alongside their Parisian counterparts and developed a style based on carefully composed images that comes close to studio photography.

↓ This painting is a real ode to culture. A young scholar is absorbed in reading. Stretched out full length on a priceless carpet, he occupies the whole picture, his long body dressed from head to toe in a vivid anise green tunic that contrasts with the midnight blue tiling. Osman Hamdi's figurative compositions played with juxtapositions of bright colours – blues, reds, yellows – and the rich textures of fabrics, carpets, ceramics and openwork mashrabiya. Hence the mosaic-like tableau that we see here.

Young Emir Studying, Osman Hamdi Bey, Turkey, Istanbul (?), 1878, 45.5 x 90 cm, oil on canvas

British photographer Roger Fenton was skilled in composing highly detailed fictional scenes that were supposedly an authentic recreation of life in the Near East... all without ever setting foot there, and working entirely out of his London studio. His *Pasha and Bedouin* matched the expectations of European audiences, satisfied their taste for pictures of exotic salons imbued with dreamy imaginings. As a young man, this son of a rich family studied the intricacies of photography in Paris, before founding the Royal Photographic Society in London to promote the art and science of this new medium. Well-regarded at court, Fenton was assigned by the British government to cover the Crimean War in 1855, thus becoming the first war correspondent in history. He travelled with a photographic wagon, 36 cases

of equipment and an assistant, and managed to print 360 negatives of the shots he captured on the battlefield despite the desperate conditions. These required very long exposure times, not helped by the Russian artillery aiming straight at his mysterious and painfully visible photographic wagon. Though he became famous, his war pictures did not sell well, forcing him to fall back on still life images and oriental scenes – souvenirs of the Near East salon-style. For a while, Fenton's pictures were the only representations of Islamic culture available to the European public, as very few artists from these regions could afford to travel to Europe and bring their own particular vision of the world. Osman Hamdi Bey was an exception. This eldest son of a grand vizier studied painting in Paris under various artists, then returned home where he opened a school of painting and founded the first museum in Istanbul. He was also an accomplished archaeologist, with extensive knowledge of Turkish history and heritage – as evidenced by the detailed depiction of the décor in his *Young Emir Studying*. The painting was inspired by his Paris masters and is notable for a finesse that draws on the longstanding tradition of oriental miniature painting.

↖ Roger Fenton first exhibited his scenes of oriental life, or tableaux vivants as he called them, in 1858 in London. Here, a pasha in a white turban is seated beside a young woman, staring wearily into the camera, supposedly representing a classic Levantine beauty. Fenton himself played the pasha, while the other two characters are Londoners who he paid by the day. He also provided the props – the fabrics, furniture and utensils so carefully arranged here to simulate a realistic setting.

Pasha and Bedouin, Roger Fenton, United Kingdom, London, 1858, 26.6 x 25 cm, albumen print from a collodion negative

EUROPE DEVELOPS A FONDNESS FOR NIPPON ART

The World's Fair of 1862 in London was the very first time that art enthusiasts set eyes on Japanese prints. With their vibrant colours and often surprising, off-centre framing, their beauty dazzled the Impressionist painters. Japanese artists meanwhile had already borrowed certain techniques from Western art. These fruitful influences informed the prints of the Japanese artist Hiroshige and the paintings of Frenchman Paul Gauguin.

By the early 19th century, the poetically named *Ukiyo-e* art form was in full swing in Japan. The word roughly translates as "pictures of the floating world" and refers to the ephemeral nature of life. *Ukiyo-e* prints were produced in large quantities and depicted scenes of everyday life set against backdrops of celebrated Japanese landscapes. In this picture, Mount Fuji rises majestically in the distance as two bamboo rafts pass each other on the River Sagami.

Perspective and the illusion of depth were unimportant to Japanese artists until the 17th century and the arrival, via the port of Nagasaki, of the first copperplate engravings from Holland. Later they would use "Prussian blue", the first modern synthetic pigment, developed in Berlin at the start of the 18th century as a cheaper, more durable alternative to indigo. Hiroshige uses it here at the bottom of his print.

← This print is part of a well-known series titled "Thirty-six views of Mount Fuji". Depending on the print run and the number of colours, individual prints could be bought for the price of a pair of straw-rope sandals or a bowl of soup. For the Japanese, they were like snapshots – picture-postcard clichés celebrating life's fleeting moments of happiness.
Sagami River (Sagamigawa),
Utagawa Hiroshige, Japan, 1858, 22 x 34 cm, ink and colour on paper

← Paul Gauguin once famously declared: "I love Brittany. There is something wild and primitive about it. When my wooden clogs resound on the granite ground, I hear the muffled, dull, powerful tone I seek in my painting." He also asserted, in a café in Pont-Aven loud enough for the whole world to hear: "Art is an abstraction." Hardly anyone understood him except for a few of his painter friends; but what he meant was that for him, the field where Breton wrestling took place appeared to him as a large flat area of bright green colour... never mind reality, what mattered was the initial vision.
Children Wrestling,
Paul Gauguin, France,
Pont-Aven, 1888, 93 x 73 cm,
oil on canvas

In Europe, those few shops specialising in "Eastern curiosities" offered an opportunity to discover the prints of Hiroshige and Hokusai, another master print maker. Art enthusiasts and painters marvelled at their flat colours, original compositions and unexpected viewpoints and so began to collect these prints and use them as a source of inspiration.

It was in Saint-Brieuc, following the Celtic festival of 1867, that it first became fashionable among French and foreign landscape artists to holiday in Brittany. Any accommodation on the coast would do, no matter how basic. French artist Paul Gauguin first turned up in Pont-Aven in the summer of 1886, then a great strapping fellow of 36, dressed in a navy blue jersey and wearing a beret set over his ear. As he himself put it, he had come to "create art in a hole": revive his art through contact with the "primitive soils" of this ancient land of Brittany. He applied colour in broad flat areas, taking inspiration from the Japanese prints he discovered in 1887 thanks to his friend Vincent Van Gogh. The local people, such as these two boys wrestling, meanwhile jumped at the chance to earn a few coins posing for these artists who arrived like a gift from heaven.

POWERFUL SCULPTURES FROM THE PACIFIC

More than 11,000 kilometres, or almost the entire width of the Pacific Ocean, separate these two works of art: a Papuan statue from New Guinea to the west; and a curious-looking "paddle" with eyebrows from Easter Island to the east. But despite the distance between them, these two objects belong to the world of Oceanic art: a realm that encompasses all the artists scattered across thousands of islands, covering one third of the Earth's surface.

→ **Every *malanggan* sculpture features a particular set of motifs that are the possession solely of that clan. They serve to identify its members and are transmitted with their accompanying rights and responsibilities. The feather crowning the head of this figure probably symbolises the powerful white-bellied sea eagle – the bird totem of the native people of New Ireland. The masculine characteristics represent the figure's physical strength as a protector of the clan, while its feminine characteristics are a reminder of its duty to nurture the clan for prosperity. Such unusual artworks held a fascination for French surrealist poet André Breton, who was delighted the day he was actually able to acquire one.**
Uli statue, ancestor figure, Papua-New Guinea, New Ireland, ca. 1700–1900, 126 cm, painted wood

This ancestor, with its blending of masculine and feminine characteristics, is the embodiment of the clan. An impressive figure certainly, with its tall headdress, determined chin and tailored beard, from which hangs a thin and extremely long, carved braid. It would take pride of place at funerary ceremonies, displayed alongside other sacred objects. The entire clan would be present on such solemn occasions, which were part of the *malanggan* celebrations that once shaped the existence of the Papuans of New Ireland, a long mountainous island in the north of New Guinea. By the end of the ceremony, the soul had departed from the body and found eternal rest. This was the moment when the rights to cultivate land or marine resources were transferred to the descendants of the deceased, complete with all of the responsibilities implied. It was also when rites of passage were performed – preparing girls and boys for their transition into adulthood. The event was a costly business for the clan as a whole. Masks and statues had to be commissioned from craftsmen, using seashells as money, and food had to be cooked – meat, root vegetables – for hundreds of guests, many of whom also needed a bed. The *Uli* figure represents an ancestor and is destined to remain in the "Men's House" until such time as it is brought out to preside over the important funerary rites of great warlords.

Easter Island is at the other side of the Pacific, a small volcanic rock lashed by winds. Its inhabitants see themselves at the very centre of the universe, describing their land as the "navel of the world". The island is famous for its amazing giant statues called *moai*; but what we have here is something altogether smaller, in the shape of a paddle – except that Pacific paddles have only one blade. So this is most probably an object used in ritual dances performed for a chief. In the 1930s, the anthropologist Alfred Métraux attended one such ceremony "Young men and women held small dance oars that they moved in unison as they advanced back and forth along a narrow corridor paved with pebbles." Some of the poles, he adds, were slender enough to be twirled between the fingers...

↗ **This ceremonial dance paddle is made from the wood of the sacred *Sophora toromiro* tree. The abstract face, reduced to finely arched eyebrows that connect with the ridge of the nose and the earlobes, recalls the skull of the creator god, Make-Make – which originated thousands of kilometres away in Central Polynesia. On the lower blade, are *rongorongo*: an undeciphered writing system or mnemonic technique used in the recitation of myths and legends.**
Rapa, ceremonial dance paddle, Rapa Nui culture, Chile, Easter Island, 1800–1900, 86 cm, wood

THE ADVENTURES OF MODERN ART

To depart for unknown virgin lands, delve into memory and give free rein to the complex processes of the unconscious mind: this, in a nutshell, characterised the exploration of innovative painters like Paul Klee and René Magritte in this first half of the 20th century. For one, it was the enigmatic signs of an indecipherable universe. For the other, it was bizarre phantasmagorical images. For both, it was an uncommonly fruitful journey.

↓ The light and colours of Tunisia were like a "revelation" for Paul Klee. But twenty years later, the Nazis labelled his work "degenerate" and expelled him from Germany. In 1938, now gravely ill and exiled in Switzerland, he drew warmth from his inner Land of the East, going beyond the exotic to create this grid of coloured squares recalling the fine carpets he had once so admired.
Oriental Bliss, Paul Klee, Switzerland, Berne, 1938, 50 x 66 cm, paint on paper glued on canvas

Palm trees, a small figure apparently headed for the exit and a few enigmatic signs. With just a few black lines set against a grid of multi-coloured squares, Swiss-German artist Paul Klee conjures up the radiant light of the Maghreb. His memories of the Tunisian medina, which he visited in 1914, resurfaced in this mosaic of spice tones dancing with strong black lines inspired by cursive Arabic script. Klee said he was "possessed" by the East, fascinated by its music and colours. In his twilight years, ill and banished from Germany by the Nazis, he constantly retouched his "Oriental dream" as if returning to a labyrinth of wonders and solace.

Belgian painter René Magritte, a contemporary of Klee's, painted this portrait of a woman shocked by the book she is reading. But exactly what she is reading we shall never know. The painting is bathed in a nightmarish atmosphere of icy anguish. Ever the prankster, not to mention a master provocateur, the young Magritte joined a new movement called "Surrealism" that drank at the wellsprings of the strange and the unconscious. In the aftermath of the slaughter of World War I, surrealist artists rose up against the "society that had produced it", championing the all-powerful influence of dreams and the whimsical workings of uncontrolled thought. This woman aghast at what she is reading can be interpreted any way you like. To add to the mystery, Magritte titled his canvas "The Submissive Reader" - a ploy to throw the spectator off course and arouse feelings of unease. But then Magritte had a fascination for the poetry and prose of Edgar Allan Poe, the American writer and spinner of fantastic, sometimes horrific tales. Even as a child, the young René liked to go walking in cemeteries.

↖ **René Paul Magritte, a magician of the imaginary, though noted for his precise and rigorous style, sought out the bizarre and the odd in his work, which he launched like firecrackers at a carnival to rip reality apart. His paintings pose riddles, some comical and others worrisome, but all of them deliberately unsolvable.**
The Submissive Reader, René Magritte, France, Le Perreux-sur-Marne, 1928, 92 x 73.5 cm, oil on canvas

GEOMETRIC ABSTRACTIONS

For centuries, artists had represented familiar concepts: divinities as they imagined them; kings sitting on their thrones; peasants in their fields; a carcass of beef; a herring on a plate; a young girl on a swing; a few apples on a table. The 19th century then saw certain artists opt for more intangible subjects, such as smoke, mist and reflections on water. The 20th century marked a decisive turning point, with artists refusing to represent reality. They called this Abstract Art.

↑ **According to Hindu tradition, the Bindu is the Big Black Dot where the world, light and energy came into being. Sayed Haider Raza naturally places it at the centre of this painting, framed by warm, geometric lines that may suggest the primordial elements of earth, water and fire. His canvas is a testament to his constant oscillation between two cultures.**
Bindu, Sayed Haider Raza, France or India, 1986, 120.4 x 120.4 cm, acrylic on canvas

When Dutchman Piet Mondrian arrived in Paris in 1911, he was certainly impressed by the paintings of Cézanne and the cubist works of Picasso and Braque. But he intended to go one step further. By the 1920s, he restricted himself to squares and rectangles painted white or in primary colours – red, yellow and blue – defined by vertical and horizontal black lines. His geometric paintings have a mechanical structure that makes them appear childishly simple. But look closer and you will find that they seem to emit a mysterious, almost musical language. For Mondrian, his compositions embodied a better world to come: a utopian harmony that was opposed, he said, to the narrow pictorial tastes of those selfish people who had plunged the world into war. In his last 20 years, he painted rectilinear forms like this one, in an infinite variety of patterns – a radical style that he intended to be universal, accessible to all. Nearly a century later, thanks to aerial photography, we can "read" his paintings as maps of global metropolises, laid out in geometric blocks, like the New York City of the 1940s that he got to know well before his death.

Sayed Haider Raza meanwhile spent a lifetime pursuing one artistic direction: the creation of geometric abstractions, bathed in Hindu spirituality. As a young Indian artist, he chose to complete his artistic studies in France not England like most of his painter friends. He obtained grants from the Indian and French governments, and in 1956 became the first foreign artist in history to be awarded the Prix de la Critique. He would live in France for 40 years but exhibited worldwide. Considered one of the foremost exponents of modern Indian painting, he is famous for his skilful compositions of concentric circles and squares, and the triangles,

→ Mondrian's paintings were constructed like asymmetrical grids, filled with areas of pure colour: red, yellow and blue, but with broad expanses of white. The absence of framing lines makes this canvas look like the fragment of a bigger work. But it might equally suggest the syncopated rhythms of the jazz that Mondrian liked so much.
Composition with Blue, Red, Yellow and Black, Piet Mondrian, France, Paris, 1922, 79.8 x 50 cm, oil on canvas

mystical diagrams and mandalas that he used as aids to meditation. In 2002, following the death of his wife, French artist Janine Mongillat, he returned to India where he lived until his own death in 2016. But then as he himself once said, "I really believe that I never left India." He would go back there every year to immerse himself in his native culture – as evidenced by all of his work.

THE ENCHANTING INFLUENCE OF PRIMITIVE ART

In the early 20th century, European artists discovered African and Native American ritual objects made by what were then known as "primitive peoples" but are now called "first" peoples. Collected by colonialists, merchants and artists, these masks and effigies struck the Western imagination with their powerful forms and supernatural, often hidden, meanings.

↗ **In 1945, Cuba was a dictatorship. For a committed humanist painter like Wifredo Lam, his country resembled a gloomy forest teeming with the terrifying embodiments of the drama that was life in Cuba – pallid masks as sharp as razors and half-plant, half-animal creatures, as represented here.**
The Antillean Parade, Wilfredo Lam, Cuba, 1945, 125.5 x 110 cm, oil on canvas

What fascinated the Cubist painter Pablo Picasso and the Surrealist writer André Breton were the beauty and aesthetic qualities of these objects. But they obviously held a very different meaning for the peoples who produced them. The Yup'ik region lies at the westernmost edge of Alaska, facing the Pacific – a wild, desert expanse that rustles with invisible creatures. The Inuit who live there gather the feathers, skins and pelts of these animals, together with plant fibres, to decorate the masks that they carve with driftwood dredged from shorelines and riverbeds. The masks embody the spirits attributed to these animals and serve as tools for the local shaman (medicine man) to enter into a trance. Enthusiasts may exchange them, sell them or keep them, but one thing is certain: the original meaning of these masks becomes distorted. Their magical role was inevitably ephemeral because they were usually burned immediately after the ceremony. For the Native Americans, these masks, filled with the powers of the spirit they embodied in dancing, were extremely dangerous. Those in our keeping today were only obtained after lengthy negotiations with the local shaman. The peoples of the Far North owed everything to animals, worshipping them for their strength, speed, sense of smell and piercing vision. To ask pardon of the animals they hunted, they would wear these masks to transform themselves into human-animal hybrids. It is easy to see why an artist like Cuban-born Wifredo Lam (among others) should draw creative comparisons between his own works and these first forms of art. He was first introduced to African sculptures by his friend Pablo Picasso in 1928 when he arrived in Barcelona from Havana to pursue his artistic studies – or as he later put it, "manufacture" his

paintings "along African lines". His mother was a mestizo of Congolese descent. Lam also drew inspiration from the Surrealists. Their dreamlike creations chimed with his own dreamy recollections of childhood and a world steeped in spectacular voodoo ceremonies – secret ceremonies that he rediscovered in Haiti, where they also owe their origins to Afro-Cuban ritual.

↖ **This ritualistic Yup'ik object, unlike family masks passed down through the generations, was created for a single ceremony by the local shaman or under his direction. It represents a walrus with huge tusks surmounted by a fish carved to resemble a face.**
Shamanic ritual mask, Yup'ik culture, USA, Alaska, ca. 1890–1910, 58 x 37 cm, wood, natural pigments, plant fibres, feathers

ACTION PAINTING AND MECHANICAL GAMES

In the 1960s, as young artists rebelled against the increasing sameness of modern life, they embarked on all sorts of radical experiments. The Japanese artist Kazuo Shiraga used the movements of his entire body to paint striking canvases that paid ironic homage to the traditions of his home country. Swiss sculptor Jean Tinguely meanwhile constructed whimsical machines that mock everyday consumer objects, made from bric-a-brac yet each one unique.

↗ **Kazuo Shiraga's gestures were inspired by Japanese calligraphy. His paintings feature big swipes of colour, edged by splashes of black that spurt onto flat areas of red. In 1971, while continuing to paint, he joined a Buddhist monastery and became a monk, thus demonstrating his attachment to Japanese traditions in the face of an art world dominated by the West.**
Chirisei Kyubiki, Kazuo Shiraga, Japan, 1960, 160 x 130 cm, oil on canvas

A "tabula rasa"! That was the situation in Japan after the war in 1945. Its brutal imperial regime had collapsed under the weight of two atomic bombs and the relentless aerial bombardment of Tokyo. It was then that a group of artists sought to revolutionise art by using their bodies as instruments. Among them was Kazuo Shiraga. They called themselves the Gutai group (from *Gu*, instrument, and *Tai*, body) and followed the guidance of their mentor and group founder, Jiro Yoshihara, who declared in 1955 "do things that no-one else does!" For Shiraga, this meant testing his body against the paint (body art): kneading it with his feet and sometimes sliding across his canvases, which were laid on the floor with him suspended from a rope above. Others shot paint from cannons, poured it from suspended watering cans or used remote-controlled toys with paint tanks. The materials they used were equally wide-ranging – ink, mud, tar, dust, crumpled pieces of paper, luminous or sound objects, to name but a few. Such artists were trail-blazers – the spark that ignited a "huge bonfire". Ten years later, Japanese audiences would give a warm welcome to "The American Action Painters" and other "happenings" (the artist creates live on stage) – having by then totally forgotten the members of the Gutaï who started it all. But then as they say, no one is a prophet in his own country.

← **A tricycle surmounted by an aerial hoop. At the centre of this rickety contraption perches an orange press, the only modern object. Driving it all is a motor that makes the wheels and transmission belt hop, skip and jump. As Tinguely himself predicted: the mechanisms would one day seize up and stop. His perpetual motion machines would not keep going forever.**
Orange Press "a+b",
Jean Tinguely, France, 1960,
120 x 80 x 97 cm, metal, tricycle wheels, orange juicer, bucket, wood, motor, fabric, iron and plastic wire

Swiss-born Jean Tinguely was an artist with a passion for movement. As he famously said in 1955: "Everything moves. Immobility does not exist. Forget about hours, minutes and seconds. Don't resist metamorphosis. Breathe deeply. Live in the present." He assembled three-dimensional artworks based on elements that he connected to small electric motors. Then he created robotic contraptions consisting of an absurd collection of diverse objects. His exhibitions offered visitors the opportunity to explore his metal junk heaps, now reinvented as poetic, burlesque constructions. Tinguely intended these devices as a protest against the bland, plastic, shiny new consumer goods of the 1960s, much vaunted in advertisements for their speedy performance. He would go on to assemble ever bigger machines, such as the *Cyclop*, an immense bodiless head 22.5 metres tall. Made from 660 tons of scrap metal, he built it with his friends over a period of 30 years, until 1991, the year of his death.

in every form. Artworks from around the globe, America, China, India, Africa, South America and the Near East, reflect these very real issues and help us in turn reflect on humanity's role on Earth.

The American artist Cy Twombly took inspiration from the light of "Happy Arabia", a fertile land planted with the tree from which purifying incense is obtained. At the southern borders of the Arabian Peninsula, the coastal region of Dhofar (in the Sultanate of Oman) boasts an extraordinary oasis kept regularly watered by India's summer monsoon. The town of Salalah faces the intense blue of the Indian Ocean, surrounded by lush green mountains and cascading waterfalls. The region was also the homeland of the legendary character Sinbad the Sailor. Poet and painter Cy Twombly, though he never actually went there, was so fascinated by this land that in his twilight years he conjured up enough youthful energy to throw paint at the canvas lasso-like, creating white abstractions on a Prussian blue background that resemble the handwriting of some gigantic baby. But then again, they could also be waves, foam, ragged-edged clouds or rivulets of rain...

Omar Ba meanwhile is an astute observer of the state of his native Senegal, seeing it as the mirror of all the world's hardships. While still very young, he painted on the walls of Dakar before winning a place at the city's École Nationale des Beaux Arts. Finding the teaching too classical for his taste, he left for Germany where he studied the language of colour before completing his studies in Switzerland. The unique character of his artworks attracted the attention of an art gallery. Using paintbrushes and his fingers, Omar Ba creates

← **Cy Twombly's painting represents the universe in which he created, at his home in Gaeta, by the sea under blue Italian skies. His lines conjure up sensations, rhythms linked to the speed of execution, intertwining and overlapping to create an ample but airy artistic gesture. Colours and stained white brushstrokes join and disconnect against a dark inky background.**
Untitled III, series of 9 panels, Cy Twombly, Italy, 2008, 274 x 146 cm, acrylic on canvas

← **As if in a bad dream, a disturbing character raises his index finger threateningly, his eyes hidden behind dark glasses. He represents the cruelty of the world and certain dictators. His jacket, sewn together with multi-coloured thread, is a glaring denunciation of the pillaging and deforestation of Africa. At his feet, shattered rafts suggest the drama of illegal immigration. Sketched at the top of a gaunt tree trunk is the UN logo (United Nations Organisation, responsible for maintaining international peace and security), symbolising a powerless UN in the face of a world in disarray.**
Act 1 – Den, Omar Ba, Senegal, Dakar and Switzerland, Geneva, 2016, 201.5 x 130 cm, oil paint, crayon, India ink, gouache on corrugated cardboard

hybrid bestiaries that mingle humans and animals. He paints on corrugated cardboard and fills his pictures with giant insects, skulls, vultures, masks and machine guns. He deals with violent political subjects, but set against a soft, visually pleasing backdrop of feathers and leaves. You never tire of exploring his pictures no matter how closely you look – picking out each tiny, obsessive detail the better to step back and appreciate the work as a whole; to capture in a single glance that mix of hard, prickly and soft aspects. In a word, to see the picture for what it is: a strange weaving together of the vices and myriad beauties of this world.

SPIRALLING CONVERSATIONS

The Tower of Babel spirals up towards the heavens in a seemingly infinite progression. At its feet, life continues, people go about their business. But looking beyond, a motionless sea stretches out to the horizon under grey skies filled with foreboding. Contemporary Chinese artist Ai Weiwei echoes this painting by the Renaissance Flemish painter Abel Grimmer, with a spiral of glass and light symbolising the interminable skyscrapers of world megalopolises – the 21st-century towers of Babel.

→ **Abel Grimmer, like his celebrated contemporary Pieter Brueghel, painted spiral towers of Babel with several storeys, each one in a different style. Grimmer was also the painter of the colossal and the infinitely small. He shows the immenseness of the tower itself but also the thousand and one activities of its tiny inhabitants: a prince and his court; an architect standing at the foot of a column; travelling merchants with their donkeys; fruit stands, artisans, porters; a shepherd and his flock; the port complete with its sailing ships and other crafts... A whole miniature world going about its business – but for how long?**
Tower of Babel, Abel Grimmer, Belgium, Antwerp, 1595, 85.5 x 106 cm, oil on wood

To make sense of this type of construction, we have to go back one thousand years before the current era, to Babylon or Babel, the capital of a vast empire, and also to the Hebrew Bible. It is written there that after the flood, "the whole earth will speak the same language and use the same words..." So the people conceived a plan: "Come, let us build ourselves a city and a tower with its top in the heavens, and let us make a name for ourselves, lest we be dispersed upon the face of the whole earth!" To punish them for their excessive pride, God said: "Come, let us confuse their language, so that they may not understand each other. And from there the Eternal One dispersed them over the face of all the Earth, and they ceased building the city." Various aspects of the biblical narrative correspond to the history of Mesopotamia and the building of the great Etemenanki ziggurat – an impressive, seven-storey religious structure that ranked among the most famous monuments of Antiquity. Built in honour of the god Marduk, its construction spanned the reigns of several kings, including Nebuchadnezzar II who vowed to "raise up the top of Etemenanki that it may rival Heaven". Babylon in those days was a cosmopolitan city where people spoke several languages. For the Jews exiled in Babylon, the ziggurat must have been an amazing sight. But in 539 BCE, with the tower now completed, the Babylonian Empire fell to the Persians. The ziggurat was abandoned and being constructed of mud bricks, it was too fragile to resist decay. So began the dark legend of Babylon, as predicted by Jeremiah in the Jerusalem Bible: "Babylon will become a heap of rubble, a haunt of jackals, an object of horror and scorn, without inhabitants." The biblical story has been told by countless artists and thinkers and has proved amazingly enduring. The Babylonian ziggurat was a square structure but it would come to be represented as a spiral helix tower, as so wonderfully exemplified by the Minaret of Samarra, built in 852 CE in the country that is now Iraq. So it was that 16th-century artists depicted a whole series of towers of Babel as stacked, architectural structures of various kinds – the images of a bustling city in perpetual construction, facing collapse at any moment, its people reprieved but soon to be scattered to the four winds by the wrath of God. Ai Weiwei's *Fountain of Light* recalls the towers of Babel in Flemish paintings. As he himself says, when you observe the world today, with its never-ending flows of migrants, you realise that "anyone can be a refugee".

← **For Ai Weiwei, this steel spiral with its dozens of crystal suspension lights, suggests the over-illumination of consumer society. It also took inspiration from a project to build a monument for an international communist organisation, commissioned from the avant-garde Soviet artist Vladimir Tatlin in 1919. Although never built, this 400 metre-high tower was to rise in spirals, consisting of superimposed volumes rotating on their own axes, each at a different pace! All that remains of Tatlin's utopian project today is his initial five-metre high model. Ai Weiwei's *Fountain of Light* is intended as a clear nod to the skyscrapers of megalopolises like Shanghai or Hong Kong, and to the Burj Khalifa in Dubai – the world's tallest tower at 828 metres high.**

Fountain of Light, Ai Weiwei, Germany, Berlin and China, Beijing 2016, 420 cm, steel, glass crystals

ROOTS AND FERTILE GERMINATIONS

In the first part of the 20th century, everything is now connected and the planet has turned into one vast global village. Rather less obvious is what this means for the critical issue of personal identity. Contemporary art is a mirror for this unprecedented opening of the world, with some artists exploring their roots and others questioning their relationship with Nature – a world filled with wonders but oh so fragile.

→ **The past 20 years have seen mounir fatmi develop ever more intricate bas reliefs, based on white cables like these that were originally designed to connect an antenna to a TV set and make picture reception possible. These cables might symbolise the uniting of different cultures, or they might serve as a frightening vision of those limitless images that ultimately engulf the traditions specific to particular populations.**
Roots, mounir fatmi, France, Paris and Lille, 2015-16, 120 x 195 cm, coaxial antenna cable, staples

In the 1990s, Tangiers in Morocco was a melting pot of artistic experimentation. It brought together traditional family cultures and ultra-modern themes spawned by the multitude of connections that were born with the Web in 1990. To illustrate the staggering speed of technological change, mounir fatmi (who writes his name in lowercase letters, as a deliberate break with convention) works with materials now rendered obsolete by the Internet, among them television antenna cables and VHS tapes. He intertwines his cables in the same way that characters are intertwined in Islamic art. "I don't need roots, what I need is a memory," says mounir fatmi, forcing each of us in turn to question our own place in this globalised world. As an artist, he leads a nomadic life and stages exhibitions all over the world. "In exile, I made a pair of glasses to see with," he says, referring to the need to step back to become aware of the cracks in globalisation that can sometimes cause misunderstandings between cultures.

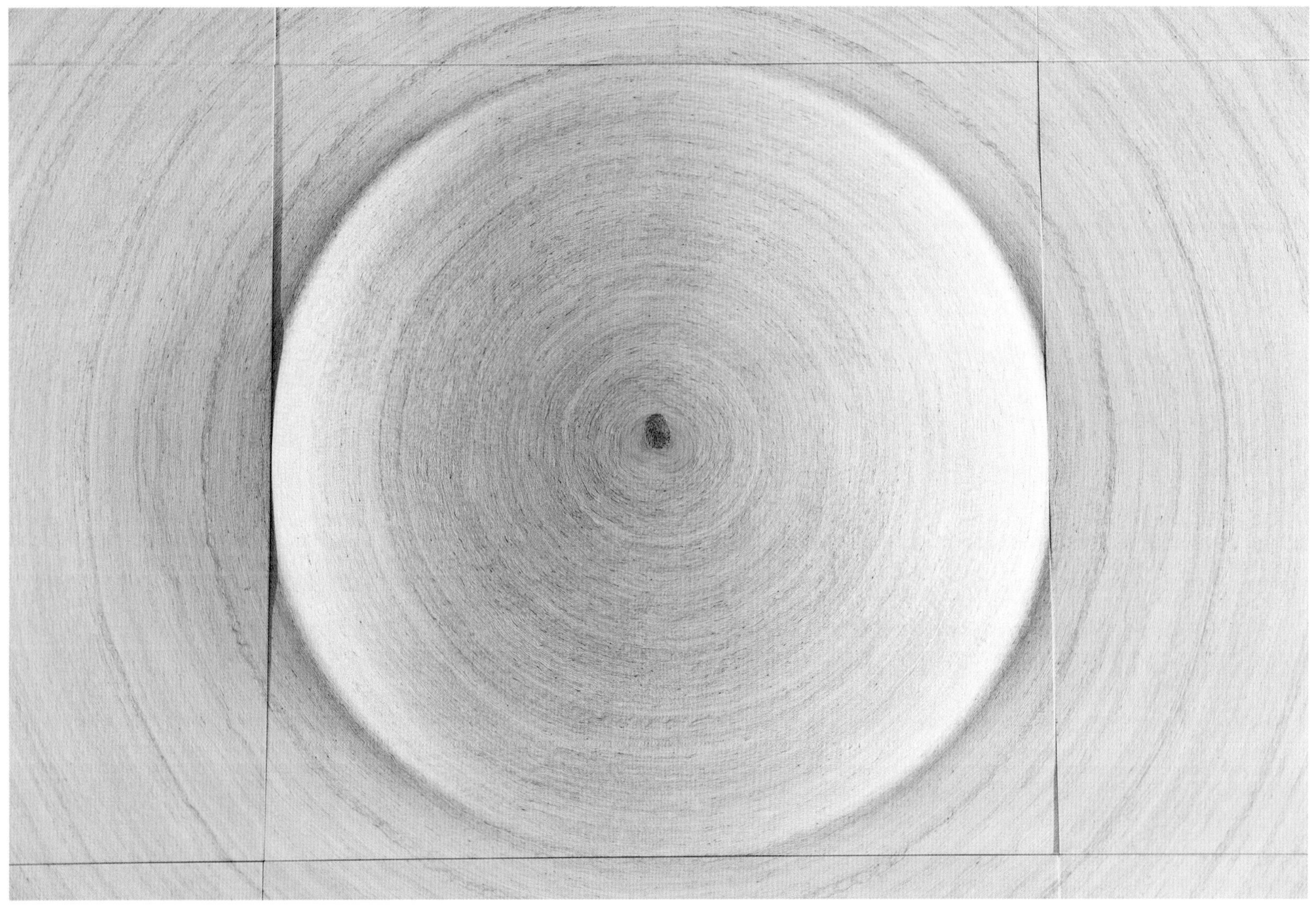

For the Italian artist Giuseppe Penone, it is no longer a matter of memory but rather of "germinations", the theme that inspires the title of his series of four works created for Louvre Abu Dhabi. Among these is *Propagation*, whose central feature is the fingerprint of Sheikh Zayed bin Sultan Al Nahyan, the founder and First President of the United Arab Emirates. This is the starting point for lines that spread out like ripples, suggesting the concentric circles visible in cross-sections of tree trunks: the annual growth rings that cease the moment the tree is felled. For Penone, there can be no better proof of the "memory of nature", but also of humanity's impact on the living world as a whole.

↖ **This porcelain disc bears the fingerprint of Sheikh Zayed bin Sultan Al Nahyan. Drawn by hand in minute detail, it shows all of the papillary ridges and furrows. Giuseppe Penone's work symbolises the ripples and waves that will radiate out from Louvre Abu Dhabi over time and spread across the entire region.**
Propagation (Germination series),
Giuseppe Penone, Italy, Turin, 2016, 360 x 420 cm, drawing on porcelain tiles

LOUVRE ABU DHABI

All the artworks in this book are part of Louvre Abu Dhabi's collection except those featured on pages 11 and 32, which are loans from Musée du Louvre.

PUBLICATIONS, LOUVRE ABU DHABI

- **Laurent Germeau,** Publications Manager
- **Amanda Nicole Smith,** Project Manager
- **Mohamed Zaggar,** Senior Editor
- **Brian Kerrigan,** Senior Visual and Images Officer

SCIENTIFIC, CURATORIAL AND COLLECTION MANAGEMENT, LOUVRE ABU DHABI

- **Souraya Noujaim,** Scientific, Curatorial and Collections Management Director
- **Guilhem André,** Chief Curator - Asian and Medieval Arts
- **Noémi Daucé,** Chief Curator - Archaeology, Research and Development Manager
- **Rose-Marie Mousseaux,** Chief Curator - Early Modern Period
- **Faten Naeem Rochdy,** Resource Center Unit Head

Front Cover:

- *Maharana Ari Singh II of Mewar (1761-73) on Horseback,* School of Rajasthan, India, Kishangarh, ca. 1775-80 (detail), p. 52
- *Dancing Shiva, Hindu divinity,* Chola kingdom, India, Tamil Nadu, ca. 950-1000 CE, p. 21
- *Satyr Tragopan or Crimson Horned Pheasant,* India, Bengal, ca. 1800, 54.5 x 47.5 cm, gouache on paper
- *Count Corfiz Anton Ulfeldt in an Ottoman Interior,* Jean-Étienne Liotard, Turkey, Istanbul, 1740-41 (detail), p. 63
- *Woman dressed in a woollen garment: protective deity (?),* Oxus civilisation, Central Asia, Bactria, ca. 2300-1700 BCE (detail), p. 7
- *Young Emir Studying,* Osman Hamdi Bey, Turkey, Istanbul (?), 1878 (detail), p. 76

Back Cover:

View of Louvre Abu Dhabi
Architect: Jean Nouvel

Page 1

- *The goddess Lakshmi,* India, Andhra Pradesh ca. 1800-1900, 26.5 x 17.8 cm, gouache with gold highlights on paper, (detail)

PHOTOGRAPHIC CREDITS

- © Department of Culture and Tourism - Abu Dhabi / Photo by Musthafa Aboobacker / Seeing Things, pp. 30, 43, 48, 49 (l), 57, 81 (r)
- © Department of Culture and Tourism - Abu Dhabi / Photo by APF, pp. cover, 1, 3, 17, 22, 24-25, 26, 31, 38, 40-41, 44, 49 (r), 50, 52, 56, 58, 62, 63, 65, 66, 67, 69, 70, 71, 73, 74, 75, 76, 77, 78, 79, 82, 83, 88, 90
- © Department of Culture and Tourism - Abu Dhabi / Photo by Greg Garay, p. 95
- © Department of Culture and Tourism - Abu Dhabi / Photo Hufton+Crow, back cover
- © Department of Culture and Tourism - Abu Dhabi / Photo by Hervé Lewandowski, pp. 29, 35, 36, 37, 68, 86, 91, 93, 94
- © Department of Culture and Tourism - Abu Dhabi / Photo by Ismail Noor / Seeing Things, pp. 44-45
- © Department of Culture and Tourism - Abu Dhabi / Photo by Thierry Ollivier, pp. cover, 2, 5 (r), 6, 7, 8, 9, 10, 12, 13, 15, 16, 18, 19, 20, 21, 23, 27, 29, 32, 34, 39, 42, 46-47, 51, 53, 54, 55, 59, 60, 61, 64, 72, 81 (l), 85, 87, 89, 96
- © Department of Culture and Tourism - Abu Dhabi / Photo by Mohamed Somji / Seeing Things, pp. 14, 30, 61, 81 (r), 93 (b)
- © Musée du Louvre, Dist. RMN-Grand Palais / Photo by Thierry Ollivier, p. 11
- © Musée du Louvre, Dist. RMN-Grand Palais / Photo by Benjamin Soligny / Raphaël Chipault, p. 32

***Monkeys and Reflection of the Moon,* Myôyo Kokan, Japan, ca. 1650-1700, 102.5 x 27.5 cm, Indian ink on paper**
© Department of Culture and Tourism - Abu Dhabi/Photo by Thierry Ollivier

Publishing: Angèle Cambournac

Production: Carine Ruault

Graphic design: Loïc Le Gall

Editor: Amanda Nicole Smith

Translation: Flo Brutton

English proofreading: Nicole Foster

Published by Éditions du Seuil and Louvre Abu Dhabi, 2020

Louvre Abu Dhabi, Saadiyat Cultural District, Abu Dhabi, United Arab Emirates

Distributed in 2020 by Abrams, an imprint of ABRAMS

Law 49-956 of July 16, 1949 on Youth Publications

Photoengraving: Les caméléons - Paris
Printed in August 2020 at Imprimerie Pollina, France
ISBN : 9781419752834
Legal Deposit: October 2020 - Edition No. 1

ABRAMS The Art of Books
abramsbooks.com

195 Broadway
New York, NY 10007
abramsbooks.com

www.louvreabudhabi.ae